BUILDING VOCABULARY
SKILLS & STRATEGIES

LEVEL 8

by ELLIOTT QUINLEY

BUILDING VOCABULARY
SKILLS & STRATEGIES

LEVEL **3**

LEVEL **4**

LEVEL **5**

LEVEL **6**

LEVEL **7**

LEVEL **8** ⇐

Development and Production: Laurel Associates, Inc.
Cover Design: Image Quest, Inc.

Three Watson
Irvine, CA 92618-2767

E-Mail: info@sdlback.com
Website: www.sdlback.com

Copyright © 2004 by Saddleback Publishing, Inc. All rights reserved. No part of this book may be reproduced in any form or by any means, electronic or mechanical, including photocopying, recording, or by any information storage and retrieval system, without the written permission of the publisher, with the exception below.

Pages labeled with the statement **Saddleback Publishing, Inc. © 2004** are intended for reproduction. Saddleback Publishing, Inc. grants to individual purchasers of this book the right to make sufficient copies of reproducible pages for use by all students of a single teacher. This permission is limited to a single teacher, and does not apply to entire schools or school systems.

ISBN 1-56254-726-7

Printed in the United States of America
10 09 08 07 06 05 04   9 8 7 6 5 4 3 2 1

CONTENTS

Introduction 5
English Vocabularies: Formal, Informal, and Slang 1 6
English Vocabularies: Formal, Informal, and Slang 2 7
Using the Dictionary 1 8
Using the Dictionary 2 9
Information in a Dictionary Entry 1 10
Information in a Dictionary Entry 2 11
Denotation and Connotation 1 12
Denotation and Connotation 2 13
Just for Fun: Dictionary Challenge 1 ...14
Just for Fun: Dictionary Challenge 2 ...15
Pronunciation: Vowel Sounds 1 16
Pronunciation: Vowel Sounds 2 17
Pronunciation: Silent Letters 1 18
Pronunciation: Silent Letters 2 19
Pronunciation: Syllables and Accent Marks 1 20
Pronunciation: Syllables and Accent Marks 2 21
Using Context Clues 1 22
Using Context Clues 2 23
Nouns: Getting Meaning from Context Clues 24
Verbs: Getting Meaning from Context Clues 25
Adjectives: Getting Meaning from Context Clues 26
Adverbs: Getting Meaning from Context Clues 27
Forms of a Word: Adjective to Noun 1 ..28
Forms of a Word: Adjective to Noun 2 ..29
Forms of a Word: Verb to Adjective 1 ...30
Forms of a Word: Verb to Adjective 2 ...31
Forms of a Word: Noun to Verb 1 32
Forms of a Word: Noun to Verb 2 33
Just for Fun: Word Ladders 1 34
Just for Fun: Word Ladders 2 35
Making Compound Words 1 36
Making Compound Words 2 37
Compound Words: *In* and *Out* 1 38
Compound Words: *In* and *Out* 2 39
Compound Words: *Up* and *Down* 1 40
Compound Words: *Up* and *Down* 2 41
Compound Words: *Over* and *Under* 1 ...42
Compound Words: *Over* and *Under* 2 ...43
Choosing Precise Words 1 44
Choosing Precise Words 2 45
Greek Roots 1 46
Greek Roots 2 47
Latin Roots 1 48
Latin Roots 2 49
Prefixes 1 50
Prefixes 2 51
Suffixes 1 52
Suffixes 2 53
Suffixes that Name People 1 54
Suffixes that Name People 2 55
Near Misses 1 56
Near Misses 2 57
Synonyms: Nouns 1 58
Synonyms: Nouns 2 59
Synonyms: Verbs 1 60
Synonyms: Verbs 2 61
Synonyms: Adjectives 1 62
Synonyms: Adjectives 2 63
Synonyms: Adverbs 1 64
Synonyms: Adverbs 2 65
Antonyms: Nouns 1 66
Antonyms: Nouns 2 67
Antonyms: Verbs 1 68
Antonyms: Verbs 2 69
Antonyms: Adjectives 1 70
Antonyms: Adjectives 2 71
Antonyms: Adverbs 1 72
Antonyms: Adverbs 2 73
Homophones 74
Homophone Riddles 75
Homographs 76

Homophones and Homographs: Dictionary Practice 77	10-Letter Words in Context 1 108
Recognizing Acronyms 1 78	10-Letter Words in Context 2 109
Recognizing Acronyms 2 79	11-Letter Words in Context 1 110
Clipped Words 1 80	11-Letter Words in Context 2 111
Clipped Words 2 81	12-Letter Words in Context 1 112
Word Families: -ology and -phobia 1 . . .82	12-Letter Words in Context 2 113
Word Families: -ology and -phobia 2 . . .83	13-Letter Words in Context 1 114
Foreign Words and Phrases 1 84	13-Letter Words in Context 2 115
Foreign Words and Phrases 2 85	Just for Fun: Explaining Why or Why Not .116
Simple Idioms 1 86	Just for Fun: Exploring Big Words 117
Simple Idioms 2 87	Literature Words 1 118
Interpreting Idioms 1 88	Literature Words 2 119
Interpreting Idioms 2 89	Human Body Words 1 120
Explaining Idioms 1 90	Human Body Words 2 121
Explaining Idioms 2 91	Geography Words 1 122
Using Idioms in Context 1 92	Geography Words 2 123
Using Idioms in Context 2 93	Earth Science Words 1 124
3-Letter Words in Context 1 94	Earth Science Words 2 125
3-Letter Words in Context 2 95	Physical Science Words 1 126
4-Letter Words in Context 1 96	Physical Science Words 2 127
4-Letter Words in Context 2 97	American History Words 1 128
5-Letter Words in Context 1 98	American History Words 2 129
5-Letter Words in Context 2 99	World History Words 1 130
6-Letter Words in Context 1 100	World History Words 2 131
6-Letter Words in Context 2 101	Art Words 1 132
7-Letter Words in Context 1 102	Art Words 2 133
7-Letter Words in Context 2 103	Essay Test Words 1 134
8-Letter Words in Context 1 104	Essay Test Words 2 135
8-Letter Words in Context 2 105	Scope and Sequence 136
9-Letter Words in Context 1 106	Answer Key 138
9-Letter Words in Context 2 107	

INTRODUCTION

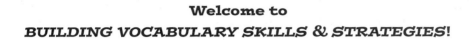

Welcome to BUILDING VOCABULARY SKILLS & STRATEGIES!

We at Saddleback Publishing, Inc. are proud to introduce this important supplement to your basal language arts curriculum. Our goal in creating this series was twofold: to help on-level and below-level students build their "word power" in short incremental lessons, and to provide you, the teacher, with maximum flexibility in deciding when and how to assign these exercises.

All lessons are reproducible. That makes them ideal for homework, extra credit assignments, cooperative learning groups, or focused drill practice for selected ESL or remedial students. A quick review of the book's Table of Contents will enable you to individualize instruction according to the varied needs of your students.

Correlated to the latest research and current language arts standards in most states, the instructional design of *Building Vocabulary Skills & Strategies* is unusually comprehensive for a supplementary program. All important concepts—ranging from primary-level phonics to the nuances of connotation—are thoroughly presented from the ground up. Traditional word attack strategies and "getting meaning from context clues" are dually emphasized.

As all educators know, assessment and evaluation of student understanding and skill attainment is an ongoing process. Here again, reproducible lessons are ideal in that they can be used for both pre- and post-testing. We further suggest that you utilize the blank back of every copied worksheet for extra reinforcement of that lesson's vocabulary; spelling tests or short writing assignments are two obvious options. You can use the Scope and Sequence chart at the back of each book for recording your ongoing evaluations.

ENGLISH VOCABULARIES: FORMAL, INFORMAL, AND SLANG 1

Are you aware that we use different kinds of language in different times and places?

A. Directions: The *formal* words in the box are most often used in official documents and reports, literary works, and speeches. Use the dictionary to look up any words you don't know. Then write each word next to the *informal* word with the same meaning.

| fatigued | eschew | residence | encounter | converse |
| heinous | procure | incensed | petulant | inquire |

1. ask _____
2. tired _____
3. home _____
4. avoid _____
5. angry _____
6. talk _____
7. hateful _____
8. get _____
9. grumpy _____
10. meet _____

B. Directions: Circle a letter to identify the formal word that could replace the **boldface** informal word in each sentence.

1. Did you know that kangaroos are **native** to Australia?
   a. multitudinous
   b. acclimated
   c. indigenous

2. The spy arranged for a **secret** meeting with his informant.
   a. clandestine
   b. anonymous
   c. pretentious

3. Nicole takes great pride in keeping her new car **clean**.
   a. immaculate
   b. adorned
   c. chaste

4. The bullies **forced** the younger boy to give them his lunch money.
   a. enticed
   b. implored
   c. coerced

5. A **drunk** driver poses a real threat to other vehicles and pedestrians.
   a. tipsy
   b. intoxicated
   c. comatose

ENGLISH VOCABULARIES: FORMAL, INFORMAL, AND SLANG 2

Informal English is the language used in newspapers, television, and almost all of our conversations.

Most people use some slang expressions in casual conversations. While slang is vivid and interesting in speech, it is *not* acceptable in formal or informal writing.

A. Directions: Write a slang expression from the box that has the same meaning as the **boldface** word or words.

| creamed | dude | nuthouse | blockhead | hitched | spiffy | busted | greenbacks |

1. I heard that Todd and Lisa got **married** _____ last month.
2. Did you know that Joshua's cousin was sent to the **insane asylum** _____?
3. Walter is the **guy** _____ I met at wrestling camp.
4. We were surprised that Rita's house was quite so **elegant** _____.
5. Our team got **badly beaten** _____ in the final game of the tournament.
6. Sooner or later, shoplifters are likely to get **arrested** _____.

B. Directions: Use vowels *(a, e, i, o, u)* to complete the words in the chart that have the same meaning.

FORMAL	INFORMAL	SLANG
1. amiable ⇨	friendly ⇨	c h _ m m y
2. verbose ⇨	t _ l k _ t _ v _ ⇨	mouthy
3. _ c c _ n t r _ c ⇨	oddball ⇨	weirdo
4. intellectual ⇨	bookworm ⇨	_ g g h _ _ d
5. inform ⇨	t _ t t l _ ⇨	squeal
6. h _ r _ s s ⇨	pester ⇨	bug

Name: _____ Date: _____

USING THE DICTIONARY 1

What's your best source of information about words? The good old dictionary!

Even abridged (shortened) student dictionaries usually define about 50,000 words. That makes a big book! Here's a trick to make the dictionary easier to use. Think of a dictionary as having three parts, or sections.

| A B C D E | F G H I J K L M N O P | Q R S T U V W X Y Z |

Flip the pages and notice that these three sections are fairly equal in size. So if you need to find a certain word, start looking in the appropriate section.

A. Directions: Circle the word that correctly completes each sentence.

1. The word (*brevity* / *neutral*) is in the second section of the dictionary.

2. The word *theory* is defined in the (second / third) section.

3. To look up *colonel*, you would turn to the (first / second) section.

4. The more you practice, the easier it will be for you to (quickly / slowly) find the word you want!

B. Directions: You know that words defined in the dictionary *(entry words)* are listed in alphabetical order. Practice your dictionary skills by listing the following words in alphabetical order.

lustrous	capacity	nymph	roster	thesis	rigor	exemption
congratulations	phylum	condemn	lithe	jargon	optic	gravitate
victorious	purport	italic	gird	latitude	opaque	excursion

1. _____ 8. _____ 15. _____
2. _____ 9. _____ 16. _____
3. _____ 10. _____ 17. _____
4. _____ 11. _____ 18. _____
5. _____ 12. _____ 19. _____
6. _____ 13. _____ 20. _____
7. _____ 14. _____ 21. _____

Name: _____   Date: _____

USING THE DICTIONARY 2

Making friends with your dictionary is an important step toward building a better vocabulary.

Notice the guide words at the top of each regular page in the dictionary. The guide word on the left is the first entry on the page. The word on the right is the last entry.

A | flatcar — flesh |
flat-car ~~~~~~~~~~~ fleck ~~~~~~~~~~~

B | mow — mulch |
mow ~~~~~~~~~~~ mug-wump ~~~~~~~~~~~

A. Directions: Cross out the words that would *not* be defined on page A (as shown above). Then use your imagination—or check a dictionary—to list three words that **would** appear on that page.

1. *flea   falter   flit   flavor   fledgling   flout*

2. _____, _____, _____

B. Directions: Look at the guide words at the top of page B above. Then circle the word that correctly completes each sentence.

1. Words that fall (between / outside) the guide words in the alphabet will appear on that page.

2. If you're looking for the word *motto*, you will have to turn (back / forward) a page or two.

3. You (will / will not) find the word *mugwump* on page B.

4. You can probably find the word *mullet* on the page just (before / after) page B.

C. Directions: Circle the words that would appear on each page shown below.

peony	perch
pepsin	pepperoni
perennial	perdition
percale	perfunctory
pentagon	penurious

devil	diagnose
devious	deviate
dialect	diameter
dewlap	detrimental
diabetes	diabolic

Name: _____   Date: _____

INFORMATION IN A DICTIONARY ENTRY 1

A dictionary entry provides much more than just the word's definition!

A dictionary entry lists *inflected* forms of the entry word. These forms include . . .

PLURALS	VERB TENSES	COMPARATIVES AND SUPERLATIVES
woman / women	buy / bought / buying	handy / handier / handiest
fungus / fungi	have / had / having	good / better / best

A. Directions: Check a dictionary if you need help spelling the *plural* of each word below.

1. **bully** _____
2. **echo** _____
3. **solo** _____
4. **louse** _____
5. **alumnus** _____
6. **child** _____

B. Directions: Check a dictionary if you need help completing the chart of *verb tenses*.

PRESENT TENSE	PAST TENSE	PARTICIPLE
1. _____ ⇨	rose ⇨	rising
2. say ⇨	_____ ⇨	saying
3. begin ⇨	began ⇨	_____
4. _____ ⇨	thought ⇨	thinking

C. Directions: Check a dictionary if you need help identifying the *comparative* and *superlative* forms of each entry word. Circle the word or words that correctly complete(s) each sentence.

1. The superlative form of *beautiful* is (beautifulest / most beautiful).
2. The comparative form of *gory* is (gorier / more gory).
3. The superlative form of *many* is (more / most).
4. The comparative form of *serious* is (more serious / seriouser).

Name: _____ **Date:** _____

INFORMATION IN A DICTIONARY ENTRY 2

A. Directions: Some words have more than one acceptable spelling. Remember that the preferred spelling is always listed *first* in a dictionary entry. Complete the word pairs below with either the preferred spelling or its less common alternate.

1. mustache / _____
2. fulfill / _____
3. _____ / jeweller
4. _____ / quintette
5. cactuses / _____

6. _____ / cagy
7. coconut / _____
8. abridgment / _____

B. Directions:

Some dictionaries include a word's *etymology*, or original source, before or after its definition. Draw a line to match each word with its origin.

1. **orange**   a. from a Latin word meaning "to creep"

2. **rhinoceros**   b. from the Latin noun meaning "tongue"

3. **racket**   c. from *naranja*, the Spanish name for this fruit

4. **serpent**   d. from two Greek words meaning "hose" and "horn"

5. **poinsettia**   e. from an Arabic word meaning "palm of the hand"

6. **language**   f. from *Poinsett*, the name of a U.S. ambassador to Mexico in the 1800s, who discovered the plant there

7. **safari**   g. from an Arabic word meaning "to make a journey"

Name: _____   Date: _____

DENOTATION AND CONNOTATION 1

A word's *denotation* is its literal meaning—the definition found in a dictionary. Then there's *connotation*....

A word's *connotation* is its implied meaning. Connotation arises from the ideas, emotions, and experiences associated with the word. Two words with nearly the same denotation may have quite different connotations.

EXAMPLE:
childish behavior (negative connotation suggesting inappropriate lack of maturity)

childlike delight (positive connotation suggesting natural purity and innocence)

A. Directions: Write **P** for *positive* or **N** for *negative* next to each word below.

1. ____ shifty
2. ____ dignified
3. ____ delicate
4. ____ frail
5. ____ hoax
6. ____ svelte
7. ____ sturdy
8. ____ showy
9. ____ rattletrap
10. ____ deadwood
11. ____ undertaker
12. ____ negotiate

B. Directions: Words in the box are *synonyms* (with different connotations) of the **boldface** words. Write the matching word from the box next to each boldface word below. Hint: You will *not* use all the words.

| conspicuous | cunning | imply | villain | distort | suggest |
| investigate | fascinated | alibi | squander | struggle | stalk |

1. **follow** / _____
2. **spend** / _____
3. **interested** / _____
4. **excuse** / _____
5. **clever** / _____
6. **apparent** / _____
7. **try** / _____
8. **search** / _____
9. **bend** / _____
10. **rascal** / _____

Name: _____   Date: _____

DENOTATION AND CONNOTATION 2

Good communicators make sure the words they use don't carry any "hidden baggage"!

People use *euphemisms* to replace words that are thought to be too strong or unpleasant.
EXAMPLE: *remains* instead of *corpse*

Dysphemisms are harsher words deliberately used to replace neutral words.
EXAMPLE: *hustler* instead of *salesperson*

Directions: Complete the chart below with the euphemisms, dysphemisms, or neutral words in the word list. Hint: You will *not* use all the words.

	EUPHEMISM	NEUTRAL WORD	DYSPHEMISM
1.	slender	thin	_____
2.	sustenance	_____	grub
3.	_____	fire	bounce
4.	petite	short	_____
5.	expire	_____	croak
6.	_____	notice	gawk
7.	offender	convict	_____
8.	thrifty	_____	tightfisted
9.	_____	playful	goofy
10.	houseguest	_____	freeloader
11.	scholar	bookworm	_____
12.	_____	curious	nosy
13.	consume	_____	devour

WORD LIST

economical
eat
observe
jailbird
frivolous
enormous
food
die
scrawny
visitor
inquisitive
runty
terminate
rabblerouser
heretic
corny
grind
gullible

Name: _____ Date: _____

JUST FOR FUN: DICTIONARY CHALLENGE 1

Say what? Your friends will be amazed when you throw some of these words into your conversation!

Directions: To answer the questions, study the dictionary definitions of the **boldface** words.

1. Would the words **sorrel, piebald,** or **roan** be used to describe a **porcine** or an **equine** animal? Explain your answer.
   _____
   _____
   _____

2. In what countries would you find **Karoo** and **Karnak**?
   _____
   _____

3. Would people be complimented on their **turpitude** or their **rectitude**? Why?
   _____
   _____

4. Would it be a good idea to slather **mayonnaise** on your **bouillabaisse**? Why or why not?
   _____
   _____

5. What kind of error might turn a **virtuoso**'s cheeks **vermilion**?
   _____
   _____

6. Who would make the best stand-up comedian—a **somnambulist** or a **satirist**? Explain your answer.
   _____
   _____

7. Which might be tamed—a **turret**, a **garret**, or a **ferret**? What do the other two words mean?
   _____
   _____

Name: _____ **Date:** _____

JUST FOR FUN: DICTIONARY CHALLENGE 2

Directions: To answer the questions, study the dictionary definitions of the **boldface** words.

1. What does a **troglodyte** have in common with a **bat**?

   _____
   _____
   _____

2. Where would you find an **epitaph** for an **epicure**? What might the epitaph say?

   _____
   _____
   _____

3. In what country would you be likely to eat **pizza** on a **piazza**? Would you be outdoors or indoors?

   _____
   _____

4. Are **polyandrists** and **polygynists** guilty of **polygamy**? Explain your answer.

   _____
   _____

5. Which would you hire to provide entertainment at a children's party— a **prestidigitator** or a **mountebank**? Explain why.

   _____
   _____

6. Is a **curmudgeon** more likely to be **curt** or **courteous**? Explain your reasoning.

   _____
   _____

7. Who were the **Kansa** and the **Karok**? Where did they live?

   _____
   _____

Name: _____   Date: _____

PRONUNCIATION: VOWEL SOUNDS 1

Correct pronunciation is crucial to an impressive spoken vocabulary!

Directions: Did you know that the same vowel can make several different sounds? Which words below have the same vowel sound as the **boldface** example word in parentheses? Circle two words in each group.

A SOUNDS

1. **short A (cat)**
   radio   navy
   animal   happen

2. **long A (pay)**
   rayon   began
   explain plant

3. **AL (all)**
   comma   walnut
   altar   repay

4. **AR (care)**
   daring   garden
   scarce   crawl

5. **AR (car)**
   party   square
   vary   scar

6. **schwa A (ago)**
   label   senator
   raw   agree

E SOUNDS

1. **short E (pet)**
   she   next
   edge   area

2. **long E (me)**
   enter   legal
   ever   maybe

3. **silent E (wise)**
   some   place
   wheat   deaf

4. **ER (her)**
   shower   here
   fuel   operate

5. **schwa E (the)**
   agent   often
   trek   gone

I SOUNDS

1. **short I (pin)**
   little   different
   girl   wife

2. **long I (ice)**
   giant   spider
   stir   include

3. **IR (sir)**
   iris   circus
   affirm   variety

O SOUNDS

1. **short O (hot)**
   piano   problem
   opera   yellow

2. **long O (go)**
   poem   ocean
   plow   clock

3. **OU/OW (noun, now)**
   towel   groan
   total   hour

4. **OI/OY (oil, toy)**
   count   loyal
   void   yokel

5. **broad O (off)**
   coffee   corner
   atom   along

6. **short OO (crook)**
   goose   igloo
   wooden   wool

7. **long OO (zoo)**
   tool   smooth
   cookie   football

8. **schwa O (other)**
   frost   weapon
   ounce   obstruct

PRONUNCIATION: VOWEL SOUNDS 2

A. Directions: Which words have the same vowel sound as the **boldface** example word in parentheses? Circle two words in each group.

U SOUNDS

1. **short U (cup)**   menu   hundred   uncle   humid

2. **long U (unit)**   pupil   summer   future   curb

3. **1-dot U̇ (put)**   bullfrog   surf   ambush   ruin

4. **2-dot Ü (rule)**   duty   solution   hurry   bushel

5. **UR (fur)**   occur   urgent   prune   sugar

B. Directions: Circle the word that correctly completes each sentence. Check the dictionary if you're not sure.

1. The word *heir* rhymes with (*spear* / *where*).

2. The word *sleigh* rhymes with (*slash* / *hay*).

3. The word *frown* rhymes with (*noun* / *grown*).

4. The word *facile* rhymes with (*style* / *hassle*).

5. The word *read* rhymes with (*seed* / *road*).

6. The word *window* rhymes with (*endow* / *although*).

7. The word *bouquet* rhymes with (*banquet* / *hooray*).

8. The word *brood* rhymes with (*brook* / *crude*).

9. The word *freight* rhymes with (*slate* / *fright*).

10. The word *bough* rhymes with (*although* / *endow*).

Name: _____   Date: _____

PRONUNCIATION: SILENT LETTERS 1

Many English words have silent letters. Be sure to pronounce these words correctly!

A. Directions: Say each word aloud. Then cross out two words in each group that do *not* have silent letters. Finally, write the silent letter on the line. The first one has been done for you.

SILENT LETTER

1. __c__   ~~reject~~   science   ~~fraction~~   scissors
2. ____   snow   answer   shower   wash
3. ____   rafter   listen   lofty   catch
4. ____   album   enamel   walk   would
5. ____   design   twig   night   logic
6. ____   number   dumb   climbed   tremble
7. ____   moist   aisle   fashion   island
8. ____   knob   monkey   knowledge   oak
9. ____   hymnal   column   condemn   snare
10. ____   lumpy   pneumonia   respond   psychic

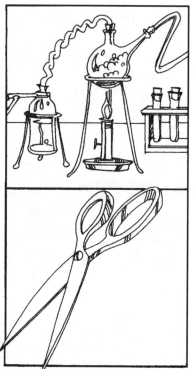

B. Directions: Think of a word with a silent letter that answers each question. Write it on the line.

1. What season of the year has a silent letter? _____

2. What part of your finger has a silent letter? _____

3. Which part of speech has a silent letter? _____

4. What ordinary piece of silverware has a silent letter? _____

Name: _____   Date: _____

PRONUNCIATION: SILENT LETTERS 2

A. Directions: To complete the sentences, unscramble the words containing silent letters. Use context clues for help.

1. "(STAFNE) _____ your seatbelt" is an important safety rule.

2. Most dogs just love to (WANG) _____ on a bone.

3. The (SLAMPS) _____ are sacred songs in the Bible.

4. The baker must (AKDEN) _____ the bread dough before putting the loaf in the oven.

5. Some people (LEKEN) _____ when they pray.

6. "(PASHDORY) _____ in Blue" is one of George Gershwin's best-known musical compositions.

B. Directions: Use the clues to help you solve the crossword puzzle. Answers are words containing the silent letters shown in parentheses.

ACROSS
3. (C) part of an act in a play
5. (H) end sounds in a poem
7. (G) tiny, annoying insect
8. (K) to do needlework with yarn

DOWN
1. (G) folktale dwarf who lives inside the earth
2. (H) the musical beat
3. (C) odor or aroma
4. (W) tell a story on paper
6. (K) rap on a door to request entry

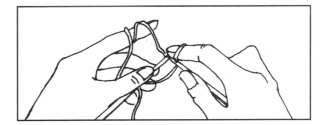

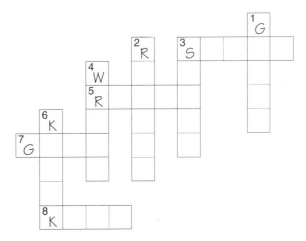

PRONUNCIATION: SYLLABLES AND ACCENT MARKS 1

A word's syllables are its single sounds. The word *okay*, for example, has two syllables: *o* and *kay*. Some words, like *moon*, have only one syllable. Noticing *syllable* breaks can help you pronounce long words, one sound at a time.

A. Directions: Count the syllables in each word in the box. Then check a dictionary to make sure you separated the sounds correctly. Finally, copy the divided words under the correct heading. Use centered dots to indicate syllable breaks. The first one has been done as an example.

melodramatic	charisma	digital	geranium
sluggish	insurance	inconspicuous	premonition
laborer	choreography	exorbitant	simultaneous
static	adversary	gerbil	conjure

1. **2-SYLLABLE WORDS**
   slug´ • gish

2. **3-SYLLABLE WORDS**

3. **4-SYLLABLE WORDS**

4. **5-SYLLABLE WORDS**

When you checked the boxed words in the dictionary, did you notice the accent mark (´) placed somewhere in each word? It shows which syllable is stressed in pronunciation. Think about the word *playful* (play´ • ful), for example. The accent shows that the emphasis is on the first syllable—*play*. This tells you that the pronunciation is PLAYful, not playFUL.

B. Directions: Use capital letters, as in PLAYful, to show the correct pronunciation of the following words.

1. laborer _____
2. charisma _____
3. exorbitant _____
4. melodramatic _____

Name: _____ Date: _____

PRONUNCIATION: SYLLABLES AND ACCENT MARKS 2

A. Directions: Read the sentences. Say the **boldface** words aloud. Check a dictionary if you're still not sure how to pronounce each word. Then circle the word that correctly completes the second sentence.

1. A **flamboyant** person is usually trying to get attention.
   The (first / second / third) syllable is accented.

2. Several of the world's nations have **nuclear** weapons.
   The (first / second / third) syllable is accented.

3. Benedict Arnold was judged guilty of **treason**.
   The (first / second) syllable is accented.

4. Marco Polo wrote a fascinating **memoir** of his travels.
   The (first / second) syllable is accented.

5. Do you have the **authority** to make that decision?
   The (second / third / fourth) syllable is accented.

6. His New Year's **resolution** is to get better grades.
   The (second / third / fourth) syllable is accented.

7. The children tried hard to make their handwriting **legible**.
   The (first / second / third) syllable is accented.

8. We discussed the current **controversy** over legalized gambling.
   The (first / second / third) syllable is accented.

B. Directions: Place the accent marks in these words. Check a dictionary if you're not sure.

1. **minute** (noun)   min • ute
   minute (adjective)   min • ute

2. **record** (verb)   re • cord
   record (noun)   re • cord

3. **desert** (noun)   des • ert
   desert (verb)   des • ert

4. **present** (verb)   pres • ent
   present (noun)   pres • ent

Name: _____   Date: _____

USING CONTEXT CLUES 1

You can often make a good guess about the meaning of an unfamiliar word. How? By studying the new word's "context" (the other words in the sentence).

Directions: First, circle the nonsense word in each sentence. Then use context clues to help you decide the most likely meaning of the word. Finally, circle a letter to show your answer.

1. Some advertisers use celebrities and catchy slogans in shoaty sales campaigns.
   a. ineffective   b. economical   c. lavish

2. Prospective employers are most interested in hearing about your bromps and accomplishments.
   a. skills   b. ambitions   c. preferences

3. When retail prices fall, revmoc spending increases.
   a. wholesale   b. merchant   c. consumer

4. Reynaldo's family moved from the inner city to a new dibble in the suburbs.
   a. state   b. house   c. job

5. If your credit history shows irresponsibility, it can be hard for you to qualify for a murty.
   a. reward   b. date   c. loan

6. Unemployed people become discouraged when there are few krinks available.
   a. jobs   b. scholarships   c. computers

7. Yuki's career goal is to become the sprictic of his department one day.
   a. operator   b. manager   c. owner

8. The head of the Human Resources Department often places help wanted ads in the wakruk section of the newspaper.
   a. classified   b. editorial   c. sports

Name: _____   Date: _____

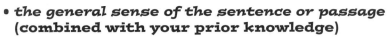

USING CONTEXT CLUES 2

Here are four helpful strategies for figuring out the meaning of an unfamiliar word. Look for...

- *the general sense of the sentence or passage (combined with your prior knowledge)*
- *synonyms or restated definitions of the unfamiliar word*
- *examples of the unfamiliar word given in the passage*
- *familiar words or ideas used to compare or contrast with the unfamiliar word*

Directions: Use the strategies listed above to help you figure out the **boldface** nonsense word in each sentence. Circle a letter to show your answer.

1. The wheelbarrow was full of **plogs** including beets, onions, green beans, and carrots.
   a. foodstuffs
   b. vegetables
   c. side dishes

2. James Madison, the fourth **stigwitz** of the United States, was born in Port Conway, Virginia.
   a. citizen
   b. representative
   c. president

3. The opposite of a couch potato, Austin is a **mobrop** of energy from dawn to dusk.
   a. dynamo
   b. deficit
   c. tunnel

4. Of the seven **slimbangs**, Asia is the largest, followed by Africa and North America.
   a. countries
   b. continents
   c. territories

5. The turkey's **fisco** is a brightly colored fold of skin hanging from its throat.
   a. giblet
   b. leg
   c. wattle

6. Unlike gas or liquid, the form of a **torgreb** maintains its shape unless it is forcefully changed.
   a. plane
   b. solid
   c. quantity

Name: _____ **Date:** _____

NOUNS: GETTING MEANING FROM CONTEXT CLUES

Remember that a *noun* names a <u>person</u> (girl, Jane), a <u>place</u> (state, Texas), or a <u>thing</u> (game, bingo). Keep this in mind, and you'll breeze through this exercise on nouns!

Directions: Read each incomplete sentence. Then use the **boldface** word or words to help you figure out the scrambled word. Write it on the line.

1. The bald eagle is the proud **emblem**, or **(LOBMYS)** _____, of the United States of America.

2. Jill's **idea** for summer employment was quite an original **(PECTNOC)** _____.

3. Mr. Calderon's **aide**, Letitia, is called his executive **(SITANSAT)** _____.

4. My grandmother calls the **basement** of her house the "storm **(LARLEC)** _____."

5. That **cave** in the hillside is home to a **(NED)** _____ of wolves.

6. Of all the restaurant's **patrons**, Mr. and Mrs. Willis are our favorite **(STUCMORES)** _____.

7. While she was traveling, Kathy **recorded** her daily activities in a leatherbound **(LANROJU)** _____.

8. Tom was **awarded** a gold **(LADEM)** _____ in recognition of his championship season.

9. The **(ONUTCRY)** _____ of your birth is the same as your **national** origin.

10. Booker T. Washington's **narrative** of his life is a very inspiring **(ROTSY)** _____.

Name: _____ Date: _____

VERBS: GETTING MEANING FROM CONTEXT CLUES

A *verb* is a word that expresses an <u>action</u> (She *ran*.), or a <u>state of being</u> (He *is* happy.). So crank up the action and show what you know about verbs!

Directions: Read the incomplete sentences. Then use the **boldface** words as clues to help you figure out each scrambled word.

1. Our company strictly **prohibits**, or (**BRIDOFS**) _____, smoking in the workplace.

2. I know many students who **gripe** and (**NAILOMPC**) _____ about the food in the cafeteria.

3. Mrs. Patrick tries to **endure** her pain patiently, but sometimes she can hardly (**RABE**) _____ it.

4. You (**LOWAL**) _____ something to happen if you give a person **permission** to do it.

5. To **imply** a certain meaning is to (**GUSTSEG**) _____ that it is true.

6. When you **shake** hands in greeting, you should (**PRIG**) _____ the other person's hand firmly.

7. **Grieving** people attended the funeral to (**RUNOM**) _____ the loss of their friend.

8. If you (**YAP**) _____ your employees well, you are **compensating** them adequately.

9. They hoped to (**PTNEVER**) _____ disaster by trying to **thwart** the criminal's evil plan.

10. The mayor wanted to **regenerate**, or (**ROTESER**) _____, the public's interest in the expensive building project.

Name: _____   Date: _____

ADJECTIVES: GETTING MEANING FROM CONTEXT CLUES

Adjectives describe nouns or pronouns. Adjectives answer such questions as <u>how many?</u> (four candidates), or <u>what kind?</u> (Democratic candidate). Using adjectives adds depth and color to communication.

Directions: Read each incomplete sentence. Then use the **boldface** word or words to help you figure out the scrambled word. Write it on the line.

1. Jackie hated (**DIMUH**) _____ weather because the **dampness** made her skin feel **clammy**.

2. That (**ETTIPE**) _____ girl over there is the **tiniest** member of the gymnastics team.

3. Because of his **rigid** rules, Mr. Cowan is known as an extremely (**CRITTS**) _____ teacher.

4. Information in the **confidential** files is supposed to be kept absolutely (**ESTREC**) _____.

5. We didn't realize how (**DURE**) _____ Todd could be until we overheard his **discourteous** remarks.

6. (**SOURGIVO**) _____ exercise can be very exhausting, even for people who are very **active** and **fit**.

7. The **massive** shipping carton was almost too (**VAYHE**) _____ for the forklift.

8. Everyone enjoyed the (**VERLEC**) _____ comedian's **witty** stand-up routine.

9. The **eerie** moaning sound was just one of the (**DRIEW**) _____ special effects in the haunted house.

10. I appreciated Rudy's (**FRIEB**) _____ email message because it was **short** and right to the point.

Name: _____ **Date:** _____

ADVERBS: GETTING MEANING FROM CONTEXT CLUES

An *adverb* modifies or qualifies a verb. It answers such questions as <u>when?</u> (*currently*), <u>how?</u> (*boldly*), <u>where?</u> (*everywhere*), <u>how often?</u> (*frequently*), or <u>to what extent?</u> (*totally*). Now get ready to *energetically* charge ahead with this adverb lesson.

Directions: Complete each sentence with the most appropriate adverb. Use the **boldface** words as clues. Check a dictionary if you need help with word meaning.

1. **Determined** to survive, Gabriela grabbed hold of the life preserver and hung on _____.
   (reluctantly / tenderly / tenaciously)

2. With a **minimum of explanation**, Sara _____ answered the reporter's rude questions.
   (tersely / angrily / politely)

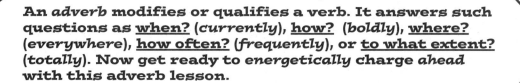

3. **Everyone could see** that Andrew was _____ upset by the unfair accusation. (noticeably / quite / terribly)

4. As was his **habit**, Manny was _____ modest about his amazing achievement. (alarmingly / characteristically / unusually)

5. The **harsh** judge saw that the repeat offender was _____ punished. (haltingly / severely / humbly)

6. Lost in happy **memories**, Mrs. Davis _____ studied the old photographs. (wistfully / regrettably / vigorously)

7. The **clever** debater _____ took advantage of his opponent's mistake. (horrendously / luckily / shrewdly)

8. The **sneaky** student _____ peeked at his neighbor's answers. (covertly / gratefully / boldly)

Name: _____ Date: _____

FORMS OF A WORD: ADJECTIVE TO NOUN 1

Most *adjectives* (describing words) can be rewritten as nouns (*fantastic* → *fantasy*). Remember to keep a dictionary nearby for help.

A. Directions: Notice that all clues are *adjectives*. Complete the crossword puzzle with the *noun* form of each adjective.

ACROSS
3. abundant
6. visual
7. strong

DOWN
1. precise
2. valid
4. beneficial
5. critical

B. Directions: Now use one of the puzzle answer words to complete each sentence below.

1. Many employees see health insurance as their most valued job _____.

2. We were grateful for the _____ of food at our Thanksgiving dinner.

3. A _____ of some kind often marks a turning point in history.

4. Machinists must be able to use their tools with great _____.

5. Weightlifting improves _____ and muscle tone.

6. Several of Mia's colleagues doubted the _____ of her lab experiments.

7. Hal's new glasses greatly improved his _____.

Name: _____ Date: _____

FORMS OF A WORD: ADJECTIVE TO NOUN 2

Directions: Write an original sentence using the noun form of each **boldface** adjective.

1. **various** choices _____

2. **intelligent** decisions _____

3. **repetitive** questions _____

4. a **proud** moment _____

5. a **ruthless** tyrant _____

6. a **loyal** friend _____

7. an **expressive** face _____

8. a **hereditary** disease _____

9. a **futile** effort _____

10. a **solemn** occasion _____

11. an **eminent** scientist _____

Name: _____ Date: _____

FORMS OF A WORD: VERB TO ADJECTIVE 1

Many *verbs* (action words) can be rewritten as adjectives (*enjoy* → *enjoyable*). Remember to keep a dictionary nearby for help.

A. Directions: Notice that all clue words are *verbs*. Complete the crossword puzzle with the *adjective* form of each verb.

ACROSS
2. prosper
5. satisfy
6. respect

DOWN
1. perish
3. excel
4. break

B. Directions: Write an answer word from the puzzle next to the definition it matches.

1. _____: good enough to meet a need or wish
2. _____: having continued success; thriving; wealthy
3. _____: split or cracked into pieces; not in working condition
4. _____: likely to spoil or die
5. _____: very good; better than others of its kind
6. _____: showing honor or regard for something or someone

C. Directions: Now write original sentences using any *two* of the adjectives.

1. _____
2. _____

Name: _____   Date: _____

FORMS OF A WORD: VERB TO ADJECTIVE 2

Directions: Write an original sentence using the adjective form of each **boldface** verb.

1. birds that **migrate** _____

2. to **praise** achievement _____

3. to slowly **emerge** _____

4. to **tolerate** differences _____

5. to **mourn** a loss _____

6. to **sew** a seam _____

7. to **shade** your eyes _____

8. to **persuade** others _____

9. to **offend** someone _____

10. to **magnetize** steel _____

11. to **inform** the public _____

FORMS OF A WORD: NOUN TO VERB 1

Many *nouns* (naming words) can be rewritten in *verb* (action word) form. Example: *recognition* → *recognize*. These can be tough—so keep a dictionary handy!

A. Directions: Notice that the **boldface** clues are *nouns* (naming words). Puzzle answers are the *verb* form of each noun. Check a dictionary if you need help.

ACROSS
1. **disruption** of service
4. pain **relief**
7. wise **decision**

DOWN
2. quick **recovery**
3. slow **descent**
5. armed **invasion**
6. stamp **collection**

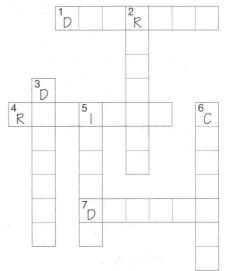

B. Directions: Now use one of the puzzle answer words to complete each sentence below.

1. The plane started to _____ about 30 minutes before it landed.

2. We will defend ourselves if enemy troops try to _____ our country.

3. Daniel will _____ tin cans and take them to the recycle center.

4. Do you think the police will be able to _____ your stolen car?

5. Francesca used an ice pack to _____ her painfully swollen ankle.

6. If you open the window, noise from the street may _____ our business meeting.

7. She has to _____ which dress to wear to the prom.

Name: _____ Date: _____

FORMS OF A WORD: NOUN TO VERB 2

Directions: Write an original sentence using the verb form of each **boldface** noun.

1. an unexpected **vacancy** _____

2. a sincere **apology** _____

3. a timely **intervention** _____

4. the driver's **examination** _____

5. interesting **commentary** _____

6. career **guidance** _____

7. a special **provision** _____

8. a booming **economy** _____

9. a traffic **citation** _____

10. careful **observation** _____

11. to have some **knowledge** _____

JUST FOR FUN: WORD LADDERS 1

Word play adds enjoyment to vocabulary-building! So have fun discovering what a difference just a letter or two can make.

A. Directions: Change one letter in each **boldface** word to complete the word ladder. The clues will help you. The first one has been done as an example.

1. **SAIL**
   - _tail_ a dog wags it
   - _pail_ a bucket
   - _mail_ send a letter

2. **MEEK**
   - _____ a quick look
   - _____ to look for
   - _____ 7 days

3. **COIL**
   - _____ an aluminum sheet
   - _____ hard work
   - _____ dirt

4. **WIRE**
   - _____ to employ
   - _____ flames
   - _____ a car part

5. **CART**
   - _____ a tiny arrow
   - _____ a piece
   - _____ a small pie

6. **LOSS**
   - _____ to throw
   - _____ a green plant
   - _____ an employer

B. Directions: Now replace *two* letters to complete the following word ladders.

1. **TRICK**
   - _____ a baby rooster
   - _____ not thin
   - _____ speedy

2. **BLESS**
   - _____ a girl's garment
   - _____ a board game
   - _____ to take a stab

3. **SCANT**
   - _____ has roots
   - _____ to freely give
   - _____ at a tilt

4. **GRASS**
   - _____ shiny metal
   - _____ a student group
   - _____ a window pane

Name: _____ Date: _____

JUST FOR FUN: WORD LADDERS 2

A. Directions: Make new words by adding one letter at the *beginning* of each short word. The first one has been done for you.

1. _t_ rain
   _t_ ray
   _t_ hen

2. ___ask
   ___ore
   ___ash

3. ___top
   ___tar
   ___old

4. ___air
   ___eel
   ___our

5. ___ear
   ___ate
   ___ire

6. ___ow
   ___lass
   ___lip

B. Directions: This time you will make new words by adding one letter at the *end* of each short word.

1. ten___
   pain___
   tin___

2. sin___
   win___
   kin___

3. fee___
   wee___
   see___

4. rat___
   dim___
   cut___

C. Directions: Now add a letter *inside* the short word to make a new word. The first one has been done for you.

1. sad *sand or said*
2. cub _____
3. lit _____
4. bag _____
5. say _____
6. far _____
7. sum _____
8. hit _____

MAKING COMPOUND WORDS 1

Many English words are combinations of two smaller words. *Sunshine* and *thunderstorm* are examples of familiar *compound words*.

A. Directions:
Combine words from the first list with words from the second list to make compound words. Write a letter to show which words go together. The first one has been done for you.

B. Directions:
In the squares below, draw pictures to illustrate three of the compound words you made. Write the word under each picture.

1. _e_ after *noon*   a. cycle
2. ____ bare_____   b. foot
3. ____ camp_____   c. over
4. ____ day_____   d. place
5. ____ ear_____   e. noon
6. ____ fire_____   f. sake
7. ____ gentle_____   g. pick
8. ____ handle_____   h. fire
9. ____ ice_____   i. bar
10. ____ jelly_____   j. man
11. ____ keep_____   k. fish
12. ____ left_____   l. dream
13. ____ motor_____   m. ring

WORD: _____

WORD: _____

WORD: _____

Name: _____   Date: _____

MAKING COMPOUND WORDS 2

A. Directions: Use vowels (a, e, i, o, u) to complete the compound words.

1. A d r _ g _ n f l y feeds on flies and mosquitoes.

2. He likes melted butter on his p _ p c _ r n.

3. A n _ w b _ r n baby needs round-the-clock care.

4. Mom usually serves _ p p l _ s _ _ c _ with pork roast.

5. Greg's best competition dive is the j _ c k k n _ f _.

6. Oh, no! My f l _ s h l _ g h t needs new batteries!

7. A r _ _ n b _ w contains all the colors of the spectrum.

8. I wear pajamas, but my sister wears a n _ g h t g _ w n.

B. Directions: Solve the crossword puzzle with familiar compound words. Use the clues for help.

ACROSS
2. propel it with oars
5. trim these at bathtime
6. mouth decoration
7. contains bills, ads, and letters
8. grapes grow here

DOWN
1. place where roses grow in winter
3. natural trap that can swallow you up
4. sidewalk transportation

COMPOUND WORDS: IN AND OUT 1

A. Directions: First write *in* or *out* to complete each compound word. Then draw a line to match each word with its meaning.

1. _____debted
2. _____law
3. _____look
4. _____mate
5. _____sight
6. _____rage
7. _____cast

a. person rejected by other members of a group
b. the ability to understand things as they really are
c. person kept in a prison or mental hospital
d. 1. a criminal 2. to pass a law against
e. 1. cruel or evil act
   2. great anger about an injustice, etc.
f. 1. point of view
   2. what is likely in the future
g. 1. owing money, thanks, etc.
   2. obliged to repay

B. Directions: Use words from the box to complete the answer words. Then solve the crossword puzzle.

| set | valuable | grown | dated | burst | doors | break |

ACROSS

1. Jeff would rather work **in**_____ than out in the rain.
3. Kelly has a painfully **in**_____ toenail.
6. Tony's angry **out**_____ hurt his sister's feelings.
7. An **in**_____ piece of art is considered to be priceless.

DOWN

2. Our unlucky plan was doomed from the **out**_____.
4. An **out**_____ of flu kept many students home from school.
5. Much of the information in that old encyclopedia is **out**_____.

Name: _____ Date: _____

COMPOUND WORDS: *IN* AND *OUT* 2

Directions: Use the context clues to help you figure out the incomplete compound words. Check a dictionary if you need help.

1. An *in*_____ is a narrow strip of water running into land from a river, lake, or ocean.

2. In a pair of trousers, the line of stitches from the crotch to the bottom of the leg is the *in*_____.

3. A sociable person who makes friends easily is said to be *out*_____.

4. The *out*_____ of the election was eagerly awaited by all the campaign workers.

5. The *in*_____ included in the package listed the amounts and prices of the goods enclosed.

6. Dutiful parents try to *in*_____ honesty in their young children.

7. The top part of the foot above the arch is called the *in*_____.

8. Bill used to be a shortstop, but now he plays in the *out*_____.

9. The *out*_____ ocean liner left port at 6:00 A.M.

10. Physical activity gives children a necessary *out*_____ for their energy.

11. We were told to wash the windows on the *in*_____ as well as the *out*_____.

COMPOUND WORDS: UP AND DOWN 1

A. Directions: Unscramble the words to complete the sentences.
Hint: All the scrambled words begin with either *up* or *down*.

1. The new police chief promised to (**UTROPO**) _____ crime in our city.
2. You'll find the custodian's office (**SIRNOSTAWD**) _____ in the basement.
3. The citizens cheered the (**LAWFLOND**) _____ of the cruel dictator.
4. Robert's cheerful, (**PETBAU**) _____ personality makes him an excellent customer service representative.
5. Our scent was carried (**WONDDINW**) _____ to the frightened deer.
6. The governor's surprising announcement threw the crowd into an (**URAROP**) _____.

B. Directions: Use words from the box to complete the answer words.
Then use the completed words to solve the puzzle.

| pour | date | turn | keep | right | grade | town | cast | rising |

ACROSS

1. The store owner was happy that his business took a sharp **up**_____.
5. We were all drenched in the sudden **down**_____.
7. The boy's **down**_____ eyes betrayed his fear.
8. The fence pickets were nailed in an **up**_____ position.
9. The **up**_____ on an old car can be quite expensive.

DOWN

2. The rebels had been planning their **up**_____ for months.
3. The boss decided to **down**_____ Chip from clerk to delivery boy.
4. You can **up**_____ your report by adding recent events.
6. The main business district is located **down**_____.

COMPOUND WORDS: UP AND DOWN 2

Directions: Use context clues to help you figure out the compound words beginning with *up* or *down*. Check a dictionary if you need more ideas.

1. I can always count on good music to *up*_____ my sagging spirits.

2. After her operation, Grandma's health went *down*_____.

3. The theater's *up*_____ events are scheduled several months ahead of time.

4. The fishing boat traveled 100 miles *up*_____ from the capital city.

5. Eric had to stop and catch his breath after the long *up*_____ climb.

6. Kristin felt *down*_____ after her second unsuccessful attempt to be elected class president.

7. The *up*_____ payment was a lot more than Harold could afford.

8. The haughty clerk was *down*_____ rude to the poorly dressed customer.

9. *Down*_____ people are forced to live in poverty by those in power.

10. A person's *up*_____ is the care and training he or she received while growing up.

COMPOUND WORDS: OVER AND UNDER 1

A. Directions: First write *over* or *under* to complete each compound word. Then draw a line to match each word with its meaning.

1. _____dog
2. _____throw
3. _____cast
4. _____handed
5. _____graduate
6. _____haul
7. _____take

a. college student who has not yet received a bachelor's degree
b. person or side who is expected to lose
c. not open, fair, or honest
d. to enter into or upon a journey or task
e. to check over carefully and make needed repairs
f. not sunny; dark and cloudy
g. to defeat or put an end to

B. Directions: Use words from the box to complete the words and solve the puzzle.

| go | mine | turn | come | stand | study | due |

ACROSS

1. The defendant's lawyer tried to convince the judge to **over**_____ the decision.
4. It would be hard for the old man to **under**_____ the difficult surgery.
5. No one can **under**_____ why Pat suddenly changed her mind.
6. Those false rumors could **under**_____ the mayor's new program.

DOWN

1. You must pay a late charge on that **over**_____ bill.
2. If the star of the show gets sick, her **under**_____ will play the role.
3. Ed had to **over**_____ many obstacles to achieve success in life.

Name: _____   Date: _____

COMPOUND WORDS: OVER AND UNDER 2

Directions: Use context clues to help you figure out the compound words. If you need help completing the words, check a dictionary.

1. The sharp-eyed detective was trained not to _over_____ any small shred of evidence.

2. The notorious gangster was a major figure in the criminal _under_____.

3. The lofty mountain peaks _over_____ the tiny village below.

4. The _under_____ helped the grieving family make funeral arrangements.

5. During our busiest season, we often work _over_____.

6. The strong _under_____ was carrying the exhausted swimmer out to sea.

7. The music store had a temporary _over_____ of CD players.

8. If you _over_____ the washer, your laundry won't get clean.

9. The toddler is often _under_____ when his mother is housecleaning.

10. Mack cleared out the _under_____ beneath the trees on his property.

11. The kidnapper's message had a very threatening _under_____.

CHOOSING PRECISE WORDS 1

Choosing words with *exact* meanings greatly improves your communication skills!

A. Directions: Write **G** for *general* or **S** for *specific* to identify each word below. Then write a specific example for each general word or a word that names a general category for each specific word. The first two have been done for you.

1. _G_ building _skyscraper_
2. _S_ cinnamon _spice_
3. ____ tree _____
4. ____ animal _____
5. ____ tool _____
6. ____ shark _____
7. ____ purple _____
8. ____ book _____
9. ____ linen _____
10. ____ wheat _____

B. Directions: Make 10 pairs of synonyms from the words in the box. Then write the words under the proper headings. The first one has been done for you.

irritate	damage	outrageous	destroy	revolting
dribble	frosty	unattractive	gush	brilliant
infuriate	plump	satisfactory	cool	superb
uproarious	clever	inappropriate	obese	amusing

	MORE INTENSE	LESS INTENSE		MORE INTENSE	LESS INTENSE
1.	infuriate	irritate	6.		
2.			7.		
3.			8.		
4.			9.		
5.			10.		

Name: _____ Date: _____

CHOOSING PRECISE WORDS 2

A well-developed vocabulary shows that a person understands *shades of meaning*.

Directions: First, add one more specific synonym for each **boldface** general word on the left. Then write original sentences using any two of the specific words. The first one has been done for you as an example.

GENERAL WORD	MORE SPECIFIC WORDS

1. **trouble**   nuisance, calamity, hassle, chaos, *disturbance*, inconvenience, turmoil

   a. *Returning a faulty product can be a real hassle.*
   b. *Nuclear war would be a calamity beyond description.*

2. **house**   cabin, bungalow, mansion, shack, _____, cottage, hacienda, castle

   a. _____
   b. _____

3. **move**   twitch, run, shuffle, wiggle, strut, _____, soar, meander, migrate

   a. _____
   b. _____

4. **big**   overgrown, large, bulky, spacious, _____, tall, massive, towering

   a. _____
   b. _____

5. **take**   remove, steal, acquire, pluck, grab, _____, accept, seize, garner

   a. _____
   b. _____

6. **speak**   express, proclaim, blurt, whisper, _____, tell, confer, reply, discuss

   a. _____
   b. _____

Name: _____   Date: _____

GREEK ROOTS 1

If you know Greek roots, you can unlock the meaning of many English words.

ROOT	MEANING	EXAMPLE	ROOT	MEANING	EXAMPLE
graph	write	autograph	scop	see	microscope
therm	heat	thermometer	crat	rule	democrat
poli	city	police	log	word	monologue
gam	marriage	monogamy	geo	earth	geography

Directions: Use the roots in the box above to complete the words in the sentences.

1. George wears _ _ _ _ _ a l underwear when he goes snowboarding.

2. That famous observatory has a very powerful t e l e _ _ _ _ e.

3. If you are married to two people at the same time, you are guilty of b i _ _ _ y.

4. An a r i s t o _ _ _ _ _ is a member of society's wealthy upper class.

5. A t e l e _ _ _ _ _ _ sends a message via coded electric signals.

6. If you want to learn about rocks and fossils, you must study _ _ _ l o g y.

7. For lunch, Paul always brings hot soup in a _ _ _ _ _ o s.

8. The d i a _ _ _ u e between the main characters was quite comical.

9. Sue would rather live in a small town than in a m e t r o _ _ _ _ s such as Los Angeles.

10. The book's p r o _ _ _ u e served as an introduction to the story.

11. A _ _ _ _ _ _ o l o g i s t studies your handwriting to learn about your personality.

GREEK ROOTS 2

You can often guess the meaning of a Greek root by thinking about the words in which it appears. For example: *Therm*os, *therm*ometer. Why, the root *therm* must mean heat!

A. Directions: Notice the root in both example words. Then draw a line to connect each root with its meaning.

1. *bio*graphy, *bio*psy
2. penta*gon*, octa*gon*
3. dia*meter*, centi*meter*
4. *astro*nomy, *astro*naut
5. *psych*ology, *psych*opath
6. philo*soph*er, *soph*isticated

a. mind
b. star
c. life
d. measure
e. wise
f. angle

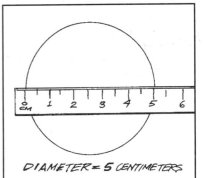

DIAMETER = 5 CENTIMETERS

B. Directions: Use the example words to help you guess the meaning of the root.

1. *aer*onautics, *aer*ospace — The root *aer* must mean _____.
2. *Bibl*e, *bibl*iography — The root *bibl* must mean _____.
3. *chron*ic, *chron*ology — The root *chron* must mean _____.
4. *hydr*ant, de*hydr*ate — The root *hydr* must mean _____.

C. Directions: Read the root, its meaning, and the example word. Then add one more word that includes this root.

ROOT	MEANING	EXAMPLES	
1. *phys*	nature	_physical_	, _____
2. *onym*	name	_antonym_	, _____
3. *mech*	machine	_mechanism_	, _____
4. *photo*	light	_telephoto_	, _____

Name: _____ Date: _____

LATIN ROOTS 1

Many English words contain Latin roots. The Latin roots in the chart will <u>cert</u>ainly help to complete this exercise!

ROOT	MEANING	EXAMPLE	ROOT	MEANING	EXAMPLE
dict	speak	*contradict*	**ver**	truth	*verify*
mort	death	*mortal*	**cert**	sure	*certify*
sci	know	*conscience*	**vac**	empty	*vacuum*
temp	time	*tempo*	**aud**	hear	*audience*

Directions: Use the roots in the box above to complete the words in the sentences.

1. All the students are looking forward to their long, summer _ _ _ a t i o n.

2. After three days the jury still had not reached a v e r _ _ _ _ _.

3. Joy got a permanent job, but mine is _ _ _ _ _ o r a r y.

4. The speech will be given at the city _ _ _ i t o r i u m.

5. The funeral service will be held at the _ _ _ _ u a r y.

6. Edward will make sure the _ _ _ i o - v i s u a l equipment is working properly.

7. Are you _ _ _ _ a i n that you locked the door?

8. Can the fortune teller really p r e _ _ _ _ _ the future?

9. Biology, my favorite subject, is also called life _ _ _ e n c e.

10. One witness seemed to c o n t r a _ _ _ _ the other witness's testimony.

11. Raymond was awarded a _ _ _ _ i f i c a t e when he completed the training course.

Name: _____ Date: _____

LATIN ROOTS 2

You can often guess the meaning of a Latin root. Just think about the words in which it appears. Examples: *aquarium, aquamarine*. Do you get it? The root *aqua* must mean water!

A. Directions: Circle the word that makes sense in each sentence.

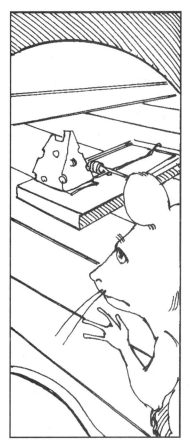

1. *sensitive, sentimental, sensory*

    The root *sens* must mean (think / draw / **feel**).

2. *victim, victory, conviction*

    The root *vict* must mean (vicious / **conquer** / idea).

3. *terminal, termination, exterminate*

    The root *term* must mean (**end** / begin / continue).

4. *section, intersection, dissect*

    The root *sect* must mean (cross / shape / **cut**).

5. *attain, container, retain*

    The root *tain* must mean (lose / **hold** / take).

6. *tribute, contribution, attribute*

    The root *trib* must mean (**give** / without / mild).

B. Directions: Read the definition of the root and the example words. Then add one more word that contains this root.

ROOT	MEANING	EXAMPLES		
1. *nov*	new	*innovate*	*novice*	_____
2. *mem*	mindful	*remember*	*memorial*	_____
3. *jus*	law	*justice*	*justify*	_____
4. *cide*	kill	*homicide*	*insecticide*	_____

Name: _____ Date: _____

PREFIXES 1

A *prefix* is a group of letters added to the beginning of a word. The result is a new word with a different meaning. Review the examples in the chart below.

PREFIX	MEANING	EXAMPLE	PREFIX	MEANING	EXAMPLE
uni	one	*unity*	**re**	again	*reclaim*
multi	many	*multiply*	**mis**	wrong	*mistake*
pre	before	*preview*	**dis**	not	*disapprove*
post	after	*postwar*	**magni**	great	*magnitude*

Directions: Use the prefixes in the box to complete the words in the sentences.

1. We used a powerful _ _ _ _ _ _ f y i n g glass to study the snowflakes.

2. In the third grade, we learned the _ _ _ _ _ _ p l i c a t i o n tables.

3. Whoever told me that rumor was _ _ _ i n f o r m e d.

4. Children who _ _ _ _ o b e y their parents often get in trouble.

5. Joe's father helped him join the carpenters' _ _ _ o n.

6. In civics class, we studied the _ _ _ a m b l e to the United States Constitution.

7. Would you _ _ m i n d me to make a dentist appointment?

8. After many washings, my bright red shirt became _ _ _ c o l o r e d.

9. Words with silent letters are easy to _ _ _ s p e l l.

10. All the courthouse guards wear the same kind of _ _ _ f o r m.

11. The sudden rainstorm forced us to _ _ _ _ p o n e the class picnic.

Name: _____   Date: _____

50 Building Vocabulary Skills and Strategies, Level 8 • Saddleback Publishing, Inc. ©2004 • 3 Watson, Irvine, CA 92618 • Phone (888) SDL-BACK • www.sdlback.com

PREFIXES 2

You can often guess the meaning of an unfamiliar prefix. Just think about the words in which it appears. Example: *multivitamin*, *multitude*. The prefix *multi* must mean many!

A. Directions: Circle the word that correctly completes each sentence.

1. *telephone, television*
   The prefix *tele* must mean (electric / **distant** / talk).

2. *bicycle, biplane*
   The prefix *bi* must mean (balance / fly / **two**).

3. *century, centimeter*
   The prefix *cent* must mean (count / **hundred** / many).

4. *semiannual, semicircle*
   The prefix *semi* must mean (**half** / part / whole).

5. *inhale, include*
   The prefix *in* must mean (between / **into** / kind).

6. *diagonal, diameter*
   The prefix *dia* must mean (**across** / line / shape).

B. Directions: The prefixes *un* and *non* both mean *not*. Complete each word below with the correct prefix.

1. Are you ___*unwilling*___ to apologize?

2. We took a ___*nonstop*___ flight to New York City.

3. ___*Nontoxic*___ chemicals won't cause you any harm.

4. She's ___*unqualified*___ for that job.

5. He's ___*unsure*___ about what to do now.

6. Body language is ___*nonverbal*___ communication.

SUFFIXES 1

A *suffix* is a group of letters added to the end of a word. The suffixes in the box indicate the "state or quality" of something.

SUFFIX	EXAMPLE	SUFFIX	EXAMPLE	SUFFIX	EXAMPLE	SUFFIX	EXAMPLE
ance	attendance	tion	attention	ment	amusement	ship	friendship
ence	violence	dom	martyrdom	ness	happiness	ation	starvation

Directions: Use the suffixes in the box above to complete the words in the sentences.

1. The castaway on the desert island often suffered from b o r e ___ ___ ___.

2. Kenneth wants to buy a life i n s u r ___ ___ ___ ___ policy.

3. After losing her job, Ruby suffered great h a r d ___ ___ ___ ___.

4. We looked forward to the holiday with great a n t i c i p a ___ ___ ___ ___.

5. The Red Cross offers classes in disaster p r e p a r e d ___ ___ ___ ___.

6. Rod filled out the job a p p l i c a ___ ___ ___ ___ very neatly.

7. Maggie was asked to tell about her e m p l o y ___ ___ ___ ___ history.

8. In d e s p e r a ___ ___ ___ ___, Ed sold his trumpet to pay the rent.

9. Your car registration proves your o w n e r ___ ___ ___ ___ of the vehicle.

10. Louis missed the test because of his a b s ___ ___ ___ ___ from school that day.

11. F r e e ___ ___ ___ of speech is a precious right of all Americans.

Name: _____ Date: _____

SUFFIXES 2

Many different *suffixes* have exactly the same meaning. This can be confusing—but I'm sure you're up to the challenge!

A. Directions: Complete each word below with one of the **boldface** suffixes.

The suffixes **-ful, -ose, -ous,** *and* **-ulent** *all mean "full of."*

1. a truly glori___ occasion
2. a fraud___ claim
3. a thought___ answer
4. the comat___ patient
5. a nerv___ mannerism
6. the ocean's turb___ waves
7. a success___ sales campaign

B. Directions: Complete each word below with one of the **boldface** suffixes.

The suffixes **-ade, -age, -cy, -er,** *and* **-ism** *all show "action or process."*

1. The brave firefighters were praised for their hero___.
2. At one time, pira___ was a common crime on the high seas.
3. Our high school band will march in the big par___.
4. Helena's new puppy was frightened by the loud thund___.
5. The pilgrims' voy___ on the *Mayflower* was long and rough.
6. Rac___ has no place in a truly democratic society.

SUFFIXES THAT NAME PEOPLE 1

You know that a suffix is a group of letters added to the end of a word. The result is a different word with a different meaning. Notice that all the suffixes in this exercise name people.

EXAMPLES: -ian / musician   -or / doctor   -er / farmer   -ist / chemist

Directions: Oops! All of the *italicized* words below have the wrong suffixes. Rewrite the words correctly on the writing lines.

1. Charles Schultz was the famous *cartooner* _____ who created "Peanuts."

2. Laurie hopes to be a concert *pianor* _____ one day.

3. A *biologian* _____ is a specialist in life science.

4. Dad hired an *electrist* _____ to install new wiring in our house.

5. My cousin is the *editist* _____ of our school's newspaper.

6. Roma, an *auditian* _____, is busy during the tax season.

7. Because he prefers to work outdoors, Roy loves his job as a *gardenician* _____.

8. Mrs. Partridge is an *instructer* _____ in the training department.

9. For 30 years, Mel has been the *conductist* _____ of the symphony orchestra.

10. The *dietist* _____ plans the healthy meals that are served in the lunchroom.

Name: _____   **Date:** _____

SUFFIXES THAT NAME PEOPLE 2

A. Directions: Use the suffixes -ant, -ent, -ier, or -eer to complete the words. If you're not sure, check a dictionary.

1. Daniel Boone was a _pion___ in Kentucky.
2. A _financ___ has business dealings involving large amounts of money.
3. My cousin Joel is a _lieuten___ in the U.S. Marine Corps.
4. Kathryn's grandfather was a _sold___ who fought in Vietnam.
5. Martin Luther King was the _recipi___ of the Nobel Peace Prize.
6. Mr. Louis Hodges is the _superintend___ of the Oak Grove School District.
7. Aunt Leona works as a _volunt___ at the local hospital.

B. Directions: Complete the puzzle with 11 job titles that end in different suffixes. If you need help with spelling, check a dictionary.

1. writes books   1. A _ _ _ O _
2. makes keys   2. L _ _ C _ _ _ _ _
3. repairs cars   3. M _ _ C _ _ _ _ _
4. drives a limo   4. C _ _ _ U _ _ _ _ _
5. listens and advises 5. T _ _ _ _ P _ _ _
6. writes plays   6. P _ _ A _ _ _ _ _ _
7. runs auctions   7. A _ _ _ T _ _ _ _ _ _
8. runs for office   8. P _ _ _ I _ _ _ _ _ _
9. removes tonsils   9. S _ _ _ _ O _
10. studies stars   10. A _ _ _ _ N _ _ _
11. rings up sales   11. C _ S _ _ _ _

NEAR MISSES 1

Some words are often confused. Why? Because they look or sound so much alike. Watch out for these common vocabulary errors!

Directions: Circle the word that correctly completes each sentence. Look it up if you're not sure!

1. Heavy winds can have a damaging (affect / effect) on slender young trees.

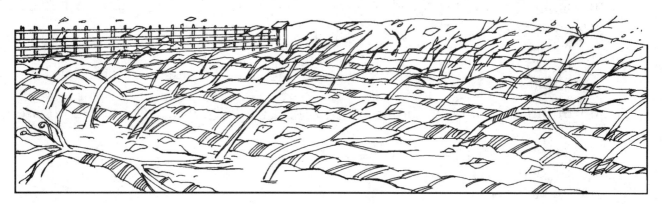

2. The fans cheered loudly to keep up the losing team's (morale / moral).

3. After a short rest, it was time to (precede / proceed) with their journey.

4. The president sadly announced that the outbreak of war seemed (imminent / eminent).

5. There was a (relapse / lapse) of three years between my birth and my brother's.

6. The teenager refused to (accept / except) a reward for finding the lost dog.

7. The crowd slowly (disbursed / dispersed) after the parade went by.

8. The country we now know as Iran was (formerly / formally) called Persia.

9. My mother loves ballet, but my father is totally (uninterested / disinterested) in dance performance.

10. To honor his conscience, the senator had to (dissent / descent) from the majority vote.

11. The opposing lawyers tried to (disprove / disapprove) each other's theories.

Name: _____ Date: _____

NEAR MISSES 2

A. Directions: Use seven of the *wrong* word choices in the previous exercise to complete the crossword puzzle.

ACROSS

1. to become ill again, after first showing signs of improvement
6. to be against something; to think it is wrong
7. to come earlier; to be ahead of someone or something

DOWN

2. other than; but; only
3. to pay out funds
4. upright; decent; respectable; good
5. the act of moving down to a lower place

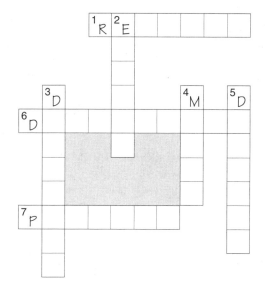

B. Directions: Write a letter to match each "near miss" word with its meaning.

1. _____ **persecute**   a. two times a year
2. _____ **prosecute**   b. to think up, plan, or invent
3. _____ **biannual**   c. something made for a special use
4. _____ **biennial**   d. additional; to a greater extent
5. _____ **devise**   e. to feel indignant about something
6. _____ **device**   f. to treat harshly or injure
7. _____ **recent**   g. more distant
8. _____ **resent**   h. every other year
9. _____ **further**   i. not long ago
10. _____ **farther**   j. to put on trial for wrongdoing

Name: _____   Date: _____

SYNONYMS: NOUNS 1

Synonyms are words with the same or nearly the same meaning. Use a dictionary or thesaurus to help you *enliven* (*energize, invigorate, stimulate, strengthen, vitalize*) your vocabulary!

Directions: First write a letter to match each **boldface** noun with its synonym. Then find *another* synonym in the box for each pair of words. Write it on the line. Hint: You will *not* use all the words in the box. The first one has been done for you.

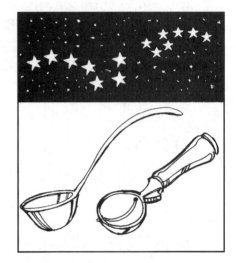

accomplishment	parable	scoop	memento
submergence	fortune	facts	pamphlet
liability	jurist	devil	wanderer

1. _e_ **demon,** _devil_   a. obligation

2. ____ **saturation,** _____   b. dipper

3. ____ **information,** _____   c. brochure

4. ____ **lawyer,** _____   d. immersion

5. ____ **ladle,** _____   e. fiend

6. ____ **keepsake,** _____   f. data

7. ____ **leaflet,** _____   g. exploit

8. ____ **debt,** _____   h. attorney

9. ____ **feat,** _____   i. fate

10. ____ **destiny,** _____   j. souvenir

Name: _____   **Date:** _____

SYNONYMS: NOUNS 2

Directions: Unscramble the *synonym* of the other **boldface** words in the sentence.

1. Two different kinds of (**RABEDS**) _____ are called **muttonchops** and **goatees**.

2. Your closest **friend** or **comrade** is probably your best (**MUCH**) _____.

3. People often use the word (**LEBLY**) _____ to mean their **abdomen** or **stomach**.

4. A (**CYPO**) _____ is a **duplicate** or **replica** of something original.

5. The **freight** or **lading** transported in the hold of a ship is called (**GROAC**) _____.

6. A country's **folklore** is made up of many **legends** and (**SHYMT**) _____.

7. A product with an obvious **flaw** or **imperfection** is said to have a (**CETFED**) _____.

8. Mike's Meat (**TREKAM**) _____ is a small **store** located between two larger **shops**.

9. Common (**CYNDEEC**) _____ requires a minimum of social **appropriateness** and **respectability**.

10. When you study (**YOHSTIR**) _____, you read **chronicles** or **accounts** of past events.

Name: _____ Date: _____

SYNONYMS: VERBS 1

A. Directions: Add an appropriate word from the box to each list of synonyms.
Hint: You will *not* use all the words in the box.

| exchange | teach | send | tell | quit |
| bother | worry | accuse | explain | win |

1. _____
   define
   interpret
   clarify

2. _____
   trade
   barter
   swap

3. _____
   annoy
   harass
   irritate

4. _____
   tutor
   educate
   instruct

5. _____
   triumph
   conquer
   vanquish

6. _____
   abandon
   forsake
   renounce

7. _____
   allege
   denounce
   charge

8. _____
   stew
   fret
   agonize

9. _____
   transmit
   convey
   transport

B. Directions: Now find two synonyms in the box for each numbered verb.
Add the synonyms to the lists. Hint: You will *not* use all the words.

support	**amuse**	**seize**	**converse**	**ooze**
seep	**acquire**	**gather**	**communicate**	**weep**
reclaim	**initiate**	**beguile**	**substantiate**	**begin**
sob	**commend**	**acclaim**	**accumulate**	

1. talk
   _____
   _____

2. praise
   _____
   _____

3. prove
   _____
   _____

4. collect
   _____
   _____

5. take
   _____
   _____

6. entertain
   _____
   _____

7. leak
   _____
   _____

8. start
   _____
   _____

9. cry
   _____
   _____

SYNONYMS: VERBS 2

A. Directions: First read each group of synonyms. Then unscramble the word that heads each list.

1. **TOR** _____
   decay
   decompose
   spoil

2. **PEACES** _____
   elude
   flee
   abscond

3. **SLATE** _____
   rob
   thieve
   pilfer

4. **LYF** _____
   soar
   glide
   float

5. **SHINIF** _____
   conclude
   culminate
   complete

6. **TEA** _____
   consume
   gobble
   devour

B. Directions: Write synonyms of your own for the following verbs.

1. repair / _____
2. attempt / _____
3. answer / _____
4. help / _____
5. toil / _____
6. predict / _____

C. Directions: Now write original sentences using synonyms for these verbs: *cheat, smile, stare, quarrel, laugh, hate, donate.*

1. _____
2. _____
3. _____
4. _____
5. _____
6. _____
7. _____

Name: _____ Date: _____

SYNONYMS: ADJECTIVES 1

Ready for some more *synonym* practice? This time let's work with *adjectives* (describing words). Remember that synonyms are words like **bald**, **hairless**, **shaved**, **depilated**, **bare**, **naked**, **smooth**, **exposed**.

Directions: First write a letter to match each **boldface** adjective with its synonym. Then find *another* synonym in the box for each pair of words. Write it on the line. Hint: You will *not* use all the words in the box. The first one has been done for you.

ridiculous	vigilant	suspicious	normal
obstinate	dismal	impartial	theatrical
horrendous	evident	lavish	erroneous

1. _e_ **fair,** _impartial_   a. prudent

2. ____ **false,** _____   b. mulish

3. ____ **dreadful,** _____   c. visible

4. ____ **stubborn,** _____   d. reckless

5. ____ **dramatic,** _____   e. just

6. ____ **gloomy,** _____   f. untrue

7. ____ **regular,** _____   g. ghastly

8. ____ **apparent,** _____   h. expressive

9. ____ **cautious,** _____   i. desolate

10. ____ **foolish,** _____   j. customary

Name: _____   Date: _____

SYNONYMS: ADJECTIVES 2

A. Directions: Find synonyms in the box for each **boldface** adjective. Write the synonyms on the lines. Hint: You will *not* use all the words in the box.

ineffective	peculiar	likeable	unusual	useless	nice
persuasive	endless	compelling	victorious	showy	main
perpetual	quick	major	garish	swift	puny

1. an **agreeable** girl
   _____
   _____

2. a **prompt** reply
   _____
   _____

3. an **eternal** truth
   _____
   _____

4. the **principal** crop
   _____
   _____

5. his **odd** appearance
   _____
   _____

6. her **gaudy** costume
   _____
   _____

7. an **impractical** plan
   _____
   _____

8. a **convincing** argument
   _____
   _____

B. Directions: Think of a synonym for each **boldface** adjective below. Write your synonyms on the lines.

1. a **difficult** problem
   _____

2. the **correct** answer
   _____

3. an **enormous** elephant
   _____

4. a **long** conversation
   _____

5. a **happy** child
   _____

6. a **tasty** meal
   _____

Name: _____   Date: _____

SYNONYMS: ADVERBS 1

Remember that an *adverb* modifies or qualifies a verb. It answers such questions as <u>when</u>? <u>how</u>? <u>where</u>? <u>how often</u>? and <u>to what extent</u>?

A. Directions: Write a letter to match each **boldface** adverb with its synonym.

1. ____ **unexpectedly**   a. moreover
2. ____ **nevertheless**   b. following
3. ____ **additionally**   c. surprisingly
4. ____ **furthermore**   d. completely
5. ____ **next**   e. however
6. ____ **thoroughly**   f. also
7. ____ **soon**   g. really
8. ____ **actually**   h. shortly

B. Directions: Complete the crossword puzzle. Clues are synonyms of the answer words.

ACROSS
1. affectionately
4. nearly
5. recklessly
7. occasionally

DOWN
1. ahead
2. seldom
3. partially
6. immediately

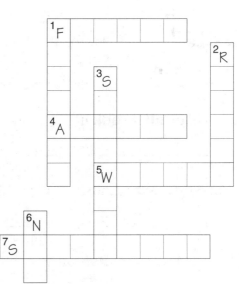

Name: _____   Date: _____

SYNONYMS: ADVERBS 2

Directions: First unscramble the adverb in each sentence. Then circle its synonym.

1. Rhonda replied (**MORPTYLP**) _____.

    eventually   lately   immediately   intelligently

2. James seemed (**HARTRE**) _____ upset.

    extremely   quite   unreasonably   scarcely

3. Lan was (**REVY**) _____ busy last winter.

    usually   never   periodically   especially

4. I haven't seen my old friend Tim (**YETALL**) _____.

    recently   nearby   around   there

5. Sue's work is progressing (**LEWL**) _____.

    slowly   poorly   away   satisfactorily

6. The rain stopped (**DUSYLEND**) _____.

    occasionally   partially   abruptly   magically

7. She was (**LAYFIR**) _____ sure of her answer.

    pretty   absolutely   unusually   rarely

8. Nick doesn't seem to go out (**CHUM**) _____.

    casually   often   quickly   alone

9. He wants to go there once (**ROME**) _____.

    before   after   soon   again

10. The judge must study the matter (**RETHRUF**) _____.

    more   carefully   difficulty   now

ANTONYMS: NOUNS 1

Using antonyms—words with opposite meanings—can add clarity to your communication skills.

A. Directions: Draw a line to match each **boldface** noun with its antonym.

1. **despair**   a. group
2. **brevity**   b. minority
3. **opinion**   c. hope
4. **majority**   d. wordiness
5. **individual**   e. benefit
6. **liability**   f. fact

7. **poverty**   g. ignorance
8. **peasant**   h. handicap
9. **cause**   i. affluence
10. **knowledge**   j. conclusion
11. **advantage**   k. effect
12. **introduction**   l. aristocrat

B. Directions: Use vowels (a, e, i, o, u) to complete the antonyms of the **boldface** nouns.

1. **monarchy** / d _ m _ c r _ c y
2. **variety** / s _ m _ l _ r _ t y
3. **selfishness** / g _ n _ r _ s _ t y
4. **anonymity** / c _ l _ b r _ t y

5. **shack** / m _ n s _ _ n
6. **praise** / c r _ t _ c _ s m
7. **innocence** / g _ _ l t
8. **loyalty** / b _ t r _ y _ l

C. Directions: Unscramble the antonym. Then use each word in a sentence.

1. madness / **(SNYTIA)** _____ : _____

2. offense / **(NEEFSED)** _____ : _____

3. punishment / **(DRAWER)** _____ : _____

4. defeat / **(TOICRYV)** _____ : _____

Name: _____   Date: _____

ANTONYMS: NOUNS 2

A. Directions:
Use the words in the box to make 14 pairs of antonyms.

B. Directions:
Complete the crossword puzzle with antonyms of the clue words.

professional	death	certainty	luck
misfortune	fact	stupidity	relapse
veteran	amateur	beginner	doubt
sincerity	birth	hypocrisy	conceit
enlargement	success	reduction	failure
intelligence	ceiling	modesty	floor
fiction	height	recovery	depth

ACROSS
1. follower
5. exit
7. presence
8. enemy

DOWN
2. giant
3. molehill
4. dullard
6. reality

1. _____ / _____
2. _____ / _____
3. _____ / _____
4. _____ / _____
5. _____ / _____
6. _____ / _____
7. _____ / _____
8. _____ / _____
9. _____ / _____
10. _____ / _____
11. _____ / _____
12. _____ / _____
13. _____ / _____
14. _____ / _____

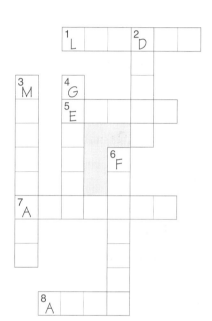

Name: _____ Date: _____

ANTONYMS: VERBS 1

Remember that *verbs* are words that express an <u>action</u> (*smile*) or a <u>state of being</u> (*are*).

Directions: Circle the antonym of the boldface verb in each sentence.

1. Reuben's company has been hired to **demolish** that old building.

    destroy   inspect   fortify   redecorate

2. You're sure to be **captivated** by the dancers' performances.

    interested   repulsed   involved   criticized

3. The relief workers are here to **dispense** medicines.

    prescribe   hoard   examine   eliminate

4. For the next month, Jack has agreed to **forgo** all rich desserts.

    demand   fetch   deliver   divide

5. They decided to **prohibit** alcoholic drinks on the premises.

    serve   tax   denounce   allow

6. Why does Louanne always **exaggerate** her accomplishments?

    brag   minimize   exploit   repeat

7. Waste material from that factory has **polluted** the river.

    forged   dirtied   sterilized   evaporated

8. If that dictator gains power, he will **enslave** the people.

    liberate   capture   instruct   dominate

9. The heavy snowfall **hindered** traffic on the city streets.

    stopped   delayed   increased   enhanced

Name: _____   Date: _____

ANTONYMS: VERBS 2

A. Directions: Unscramble the word to complete each pair of antonyms.

1. whisper / **(TOUSH)** _____

2. weep / **(HUGAL)** _____

3. survive / **(RESHIP)** _____

4. boil / **(REZFEE)** _____

5. question / **(RESWAN)** _____

6. conceal / **(AVERLE)** _____

7. remove / **(PLAPY)** _____

8. remember / **(EFTROG)** _____

9. raise / **(REWOL)** _____

10. descend / **(DANCES)** _____

B. Directions: Complete the crossword puzzle with antonyms of the clue words.

ACROSS
2. criticize
4. double
6. deny
7. advance

DOWN
1. reject
3. conceal
4. continue
5. frown

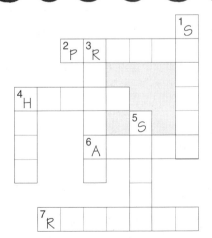

Name: _____   Date: _____

ANTONYMS: ADJECTIVES 1

Remember that adjectives describe nouns and pronouns. The often tell how many or what kind.

A. Directions: Add vowels *(a, e, i, o, u)* to complete the antonyms of the **boldface** adjectives.

1. This bread is **fresh**, but that bread is s t _ l _ .

2. Newscasters should be **neutral**, rather than b _ _ s _ d, about the stories they report.

3. Although some customers were **complimentary** of the waiter's service, others were c r _ t _ c _ l.

4. Does that math problem seem to be **simple** or c _ m p l _ x?

5. That woman's **haughty** manners intimidate h _ m b l _ people.

6. There is nothing c _ m _ c about a **tragic** situation.

7. One brother is very **brawny**, but the other is quite s c r _ w n y.

8. Their b _ _ s t _ r _ _ s behavior was out of place at the **sedate** tea party.

B. Directions: Find an antonym in the box for each **boldface** adjective. Write it on the line.

| punctual | unusual | feasible | exciting | vulnerable | flexible | immaculate | superior |

1. **invincible** / _____
2. **humdrum** / _____
3. **inferior** / _____
4. **customary** / _____
5. **rigid** / _____
6. **filthy** / _____
7. **tardy** / _____
8. **impractical** / _____

Name: _____   Date: _____

ANTONYMS: ADJECTIVES 2

A. Directions: Unscramble the adjectives to complete each pair of *antonyms*.

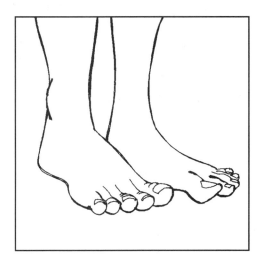

1. true / **(SELAF)** _____

2. sour / **(WESTE)** _____

3. phony / **(NINEGUE)** _____

4. worse / **(TRETEB)** _____

5. flawed / **(CREFTEP)** _____

6. crooked / **(RIGHATTS)** _____

7. partial / **(RENTIE)** _____

8. mild / **(REVSEE)** _____

9. smooth / **(HOGUR)** _____

10. unusual / **(RONLAM)** _____

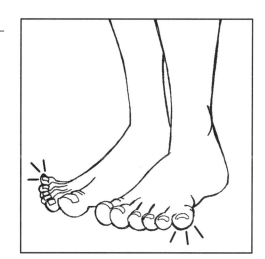

B. Directions: Complete the crossword puzzle with antonyms of the clue words.

ACROSS
1. bald
3. repulsive
6. busy
7. found
8. difficult

DOWN
1. beneficial
2. wholesale
4. occupied
5. sturdy

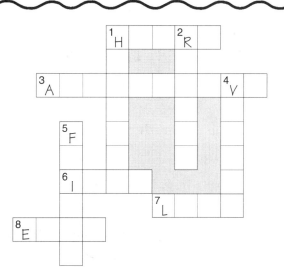

ANTONYMS: ADVERBS 1

Remember that *adverbs* modify verbs, adjectives, or other adverbs.

A. Directions: Find an *antonym* (word that means the opposite) in the box for each **boldface** adverb. Write it on the line. Hint: You will *not* use all the words.

| eagerly | irregularly | initially | repeatedly | in |
| severely | eventually | rudely | artificially | up |

1. Eric was **slightly** (_____) injured in the car accident.
2. Allie was **once** (_____) bothered by telemarketers.
3. Brad said that he would be home **soon** (_____).
4. Nicole responded **graciously** (_____) to Karen's invitation.
5. Those peaches were ripened **naturally** (_____).
6. Randy answered the question very **reluctantly** (_____).
7. Grace **finally** (_____) agreed with the plan.
8. The sun goes **down** (_____) about 7:00 P.M.
9. New editions of that book come out **periodically** (_____).

B. Directions: Complete the puzzle with antonyms of the **boldface** adverbs.

ACROSS
3. He's **always** late!
4. I'll be there **tomorrow**.
5. See me **beforehand**.
7. She spoke **deceptively**.

DOWN
1. I was **less** interested.
2. He drove me right **here**.
3. It seems to be **everywhere**.
6. He will meet you **now**.

ANTONYMS: ADVERBS 2

A. Directions: Sort the adverbs in the box to match 10 pairs of *antonyms* (words with opposite meanings). Write them on the lines. One pair has been done for you.

illegally	calmly	nowhere	recklessly	mildly
vigorously	keenly	secretly	frantically	lazily
cautiously	firmly	somewhere	specifically	openly
partially	wholly	generally	loosely	lawfully

1. *partially*
   wholly
2. ___
3. ___
4. ___
5. ___
6. ___
7. ___
8. ___
9. ___
10. ___

B. Directions: Complete the crossword puzzle with antonyms of the **boldface** adverbs.

ACROSS
4. arrived **late**
6. responded **powerfully**
8. do it **sometime**
9. scheduled **tomorrow**
10. reacted **foolishly**

DOWN
1. **never** abandon
2. **specifically** provide
3. came **quickly**
5. spoke **coldly**
7. **richly** rewarded

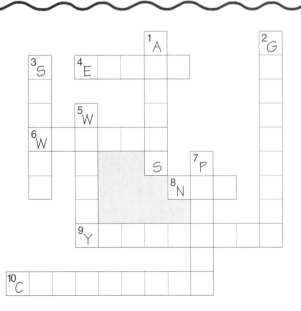

Name: ___ Date: ___

HOMOPHONES

Homophones are words like see and sea. The two words sound exactly alike, but they have different meanings and spellings. When you're writing, be sure you use the word you want instead of its "sound-alike"!

A. Directions: Say the words aloud. Then write a homophone next to each word.

1. heard / _____
2. sail / _____
3. dough / _____
4. oar / _____
5. minor / _____
6. eight / _____
7. hair / _____
8. sore / _____
9. steel / _____

B. Directions: Complete the crossword puzzle with homophones for the **boldface** words.

ACROSS

2. a **bridal** veil
5. **guessed** the answer
6. tie a **knot**
8. a pink **flower**
10. your big **toe**
11. poked a **hole**

DOWN

1. flew a **plane**
3. a big red **rose**
4. **our** wedding vows
7. **through** the air
8. a **foul** odor
9. **knew** him well

C. Directions: Circle three homophone errors in each sentence. Then rewrite the sentences correctly on the lines.

1. Are ewe the air to that grate fortune?
   _____

2. Eye was afraid of the bare's sharp clause.
   _____

3. Wood you be able to lone me sum money?
   _____

Name: _____   Date: _____

74 Building Vocabulary Skills and Strategies, Level 8 • Saddleback Publishing, Inc. ©2004 • 3 Watson, Irvine, CA 92618 • Phone (888) SDL-BACK • www.sdlback.com

HOMOPHONE RIDDLES

Now have some fun with homophones! Use the example below and your imagination to solve the riddles.

EXAMPLE: What would you call a naked grizzly? a _bare_ _bear_

A. Directions: Use vowels (a, e, i, o, u) to fill in the blanks.

What would you call . . .

1. rabbit fur? h _ r   h _ _ r
2. a sea mammal's cry? wh _ l _   w _ _ l
3. an undecorated jet? p l _ _ n   p l _ n _
4. a young coal digger? m _ n _ r   m _ n _ r
5. a decaying turkey? f _ _ l   f _ w l
6. an insect uncle's wife? _ n t   _ _ n t
7. a masculine letter? m _ l _   m _ _ l

B. Directions: Now solve the riddles by using only the first letters as clues.

What would you call . . .

1. a more daring rock? b_____ b_____
2. a genuine spool? r_____ r_____
3. an uninterested plank? b_____ b_____
4. a lone spirit? s_____ s_____
5. Congressional money? c_____ c_____
6. an improved gambler? b_____ b_____

HOMOGRAPHS

Words called *homographs* look exactly alike—but they have <u>different</u> meanings.

EXAMPLE: *fly* 1. an insect; 2. to move through the air

A. Directions: Unscramble the homographs that match each definition below. The first one has been done for you.

1. (KRAB) __bark__:
   a. sound a dog makes
   b. tree covering

2. (HEDI) _____:
   a. to keep out of sight
   b. animal skin

3. (MAPL) _____:
   a. inside of hand
   b. kind of tree

4. (FOAL) _____:
   a. shaped as bread
   b. to be idle

5. (NALE) _____:
   a. not fat
   b. to stand at a slant

6. (EMIN) _____:
   a. belonging to me
   b. hole made in the earth to reveal ores

7. (LOES) _____:
   a. type of fish
   b. only

8. (KILE) _____:
   a. be pleased with
   b. similar to

B. Directions: Write homographs to find the answer to the riddle (reads top to bottom). Use the definitions as clues. The first one has been done for you.

RIDDLE: What do homographs have in common?

1. sled dog; big and strong
2. 16 ounces; use a hammer
3. show the way; metallic element
4. to jump over; storehouse for valuables
5. ugly dwarf; method of fishing
6. unmarried woman; fail to hit
7. dried fruit; to cut or trim
8. not heavy; not dark

1. h u **s** k y
2. _ _ _ _ _
3. _ _ _ _
4. _ _ _ _ _
5. _ _ _ _ _
6. _ _ _ _
7. _ _ _ _ _
8. _ _ _ _ _

Name: _____ Date: _____

HOMOPHONES AND HOMOGRAPHS: DICTIONARY PRACTICE

A. Directions: First write the *homophone* for each **boldface** word. Then write a brief definition of the homophone you added. Check a dictionary if you need help.

1. We **ate** dinner. _____ : _____

2. Pay the sales **tax**. _____ : _____

3. He **won** the race. _____ : _____

4. Let's meet next **week**. _____ : _____

5. **Wrap** the package. _____ : _____

6. Fly the kite **higher**. _____ : _____

7. You come, **too**. _____ : _____

8. **We'll** have fun. _____ : _____

B. Directions: Write two sentences showing each meaning of the **boldface** *homographs*. The first one has been done for you. Check a dictionary if you need help.

1. **stalk** (noun) *The stalk is the stem of a plant.*

   stalk (verb) *If you stalk people, you secretly follow them.*

2. **will** (noun) _____

   will (verb) _____

3. **pine** (noun) _____

   pine (verb) _____

4. **pupil** (noun) _____

   pupil (noun) _____

Name: _____   Date: _____

Recognizing Acronyms 1

Hey, guys! TGIF! I'm outta here!

An *acronym* is a word formed by the first letters, or first syllables, of two or more words. The word *radar*, for example, is an acronym formed from "<u>ra</u>dio <u>d</u>etecting <u>a</u>nd <u>r</u>anging."

Directions: Circle a letter to show the meaning of each acronym. Check a dictionary if you're not sure.

1. In order to recover, the injured dog will need a lot of TLC.
   a. tender, loving care
   b. tough, loyal companionship

2. When I asked her where she was going, she rudely said, "MYOB!"
   a. make your own bed
   b. mind your own business

3. Unfortunately, the accident victim was DOA in the emergency room.
   a. dead on arrival
   b. dying of anemia

4. Rosalind sometimes orders a BLT sandwich for lunch.
   a. bacon, lettuce, and tomato
   b. beef, liverwurst, and turkey

5. The inscription on that old tombstone says, *Elias Smith, RIP.*
   a. residing in paradise
   b. rest in peace

6. Mr. Cooper claims to have seen a UFO hovering over his house.
   a. unbelievably fat owl
   b. unidentified flying object

7. Anna Syms has the highest IQ of anyone in our class.
   a. inherited quality
   b. intelligence quotient

8. At weekend parties, Roger sometimes works as a DJ.
   a. disc jockey
   b. dormitory janitor

Name: _____   Date: _____

RECOGNIZING ACRONYMS 2

A. Directions: Draw a line to match each acronym with its meaning.

1. SUV
2. POW
3. CPA
4. laser
5. ZIP
6. VIP

a. light amplification by stimulated emission of radiation
b. sport utility vehicle
c. zone improvement plan
d. certified public accountant
e. very important person
f. prisoner of war

B. Directions: Write the meanings of the acronyms on the lines. Check a dictionary if you need help.

1. ASAP _____
2. GI _____
3. RAM _____
4. SOS _____
5. KKK _____
6. Nazi _____

C. Directions: Complete the crossword puzzle with the acronyms for U.S. government departments, bureaus, or alliances.

ACROSS
2. Strategic Arms Limitation Talks
3. National Aeronautics and Space Administration
4. Food and Drug Administration
6. Organization of Petroleum Exporting Countries
8. Internal Revenue Service
9. Social Security Administration

DOWN
1. Occupational Safety and Health Administration
3. North Atlantic Treaty Organization
4. Federal Bureau of Investigation
5. Organization of American States
7. Central Intelligence Agency

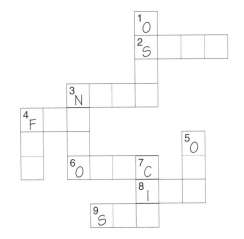

CLIPPED WORDS 1

Many English words have been shortened or "clipped" by common use.

A. Directions: Write out the complete form of the clipped words shown in **boldface**.

1. the **carbs** in your diet
   _____

2. rent a **limo**
   _____

3. a customer service **rep**
   _____

4. a Vietnam **vet**
   _____

5. Jane's **dorm** room
   _____

6. a quarter-pound **burger**
   _____

7. raided the **fridge**
   _____

8. the chemistry **lab**
   _____

B. Directions: Now write the clipped form of each **boldface** word.

1. brand new **bicycle** _____

2. gallon of **gasoline** _____

3. rent a **tuxedo** _____

4. took a **taxicab** _____

5. booed the **umpire** _____

6. captured the **perpetrator** _____

7. the world **champion** _____

8. a high school **graduate** _____

Name: _____   Date: _____

80 Building Vocabulary Skills and Strategies, Level 8 • Saddleback Publishing, Inc. ©2004 • 3 Watson, Irvine, CA 92618 • Phone (888) SDL-BACK • www.sdlback.com

CLIPPED WORDS 2

A. Directions: Solve the crossword puzzle. Answers are the complete forms of the **boldface** clipped words.

ACROSS
1. bought his own **plane**
4. a true Yankees **fan**
7. an imprisoned **con**
8. a dance in the **gym**

DOWN
2. sick with **flu**
3. the Fancy Food **Mart**
5. hire a **teen**
6. **Miss** Mary Murphy

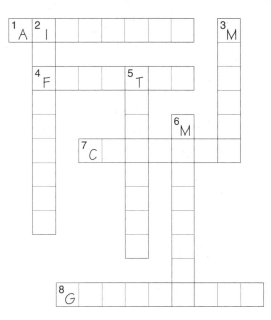

B. Directions: Use vowels (a, e, i, o, u) to complete the longer form of each **boldface** clipped word.

1. The **ref** called a foul on our best player.   r _ f _ r _ _

2. Jesse sent an email **memo** to his boss.   m _ m _ r _ n d _ m

3. Natalie has a **math exam** tomorrow morning.
   m _ t h _ m _ t _ c s   _ x _ m _ n _ t _ _ n

4. The audience cheered loudly for the **pop** singing star.   p _ p _ l _ r

5. Mike's new pet is a black **Lab** puppy.   L _ b r _ d _ r

6. Tatiana's dad is a business **exec**, and Shanika's dad is a **prof** at the university.   _ x _ c _ t _ v _   p r _ f _ s s _ r

Name: _____ **Date:** _____

WORD FAMILIES: -OLOGY AND -PHOBIA 1

The suffix -ology means "the science of" or "the study of."

A. Directions:

The names of many branches of medicine end in *-ology*. Use words from the box to identify the focus of each medical specialty. Hint: You will *not* use all the words in the box. Check a dictionary if you need help.

diseases	nerves	tendons
skin	poisons	women
eyes	kidneys	drugs
heart	bones	mind
blood	veins	knees

1. ophthalmology: _____
2. toxicology: _____
3. psychology: _____
4. gynecology: _____
5. dermatology: _____
6. cardiology: _____
7. nephrology: _____
8. urology: _____
9. pathology: _____
10. pharmacology: _____

B. Directions:

Use the clues to help you solve the crossword puzzle. Each answer names the focus of a field of study. Check a dictionary if you need help.

ACROSS
1. etymology
5. seismology
6. audiology
9. sociology
10. ornithology

DOWN
2. herpetology
3. paleontology
4. meteorology
7. entomology
8. theology

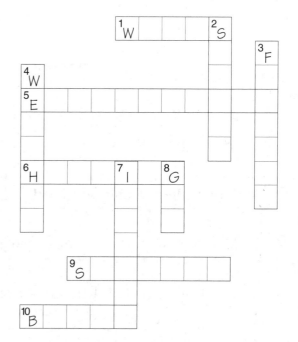

Name: _____ Date: _____

WORD FAMILIES: -OLOGY AND -PHOBIA 2

Are you unreasonably afraid of something? You're *phobic*! This lesson will acquaint you with an interesting list of various phobias.

Directions: Circle a letter to identify the focus of each **boldface** phobia.

Hint 1: Context clues can help you make a good guess.
Hint 2: Think about the meaning of the word's root.

To be sure, check a dictionary.

1. Because she is terrified of tiny rodents, Muriel suffers from **musophobia**.
   a. roaches
   b. mice
   c. spiders

2. Brandon, a victim of **claustrophobia**, would rather climb the stairs than take the elevator.
   a. heights
   b. electricity
   c. closed spaces

3. Wendy, who has **nyctophobia**, always makes sure that she's indoors at dusk.
   a. night watchmen
   b. darkness
   c. streetlights

4. Marta's **brontophobia** requires her to wear earplugs whenever it rains.
   a. thunder
   b. lightning
   c. earaches

5. Kent, who suffers from **xenophobia**, is very uncomfortable around people he doesn't know well.
   a. bullies
   b. foreigners
   c. strangers

6. Because of her **ophidiophobia**, Katya would never go hiking in the wilderness.
   a. snipers
   b. snakes
   c. sunshine

7. Dave's **necrophobia** makes it impossible for him to join the family's mortuary business.
   a. death
   b. coffins
   c. graves

8. **Aquaphobia** prevents Ricky from enjoying sports such as swimming and fishing.
   a. rafts
   b. water
   c. aquaplanes

FOREIGN WORDS AND PHRASES 1

Many words and phrases from other languages are commonly used by educated English-speakers.

Directions: Use context clues to help you figure out the meaning of the **boldface** Latin words and phrases. Check a dictionary if you need help. Circle a letter to show your answer.

1. Melissa glanced at her watch and cried out, "**Tempus fugit**!" as she dashed out the door.
   a. "Haste makes waste!"
   b. "Time flies!"
   c. "I forgot something!"

2. Old Dr. Clarke is professor **emeritus** of our college's English Department.
   a. retired after long service
   b. the department chairman
   c. an emergency substitute

3. "**Caveat emptor**" is a good guideline to remember if a product seems suspiciously inexpensive.
   a. One day at a time.
   b. Thrift is wealth.
   c. Let the buyer beware.

4. After giving the reporter information for a story, the police detective expected **quid pro quo**.
   a. something done in exchange
   b. a flattering news story
   c. freedom of the press

5. The **sine qua non** of a first-rate amusement park is a great roller coaster.
   a. special treat
   b. essential thing
   c. sign of success

6. The company is pleased with Jed's performance and **vice versa**.
   a. Jed is pleased with the company.
   b. is confident of the future
   c. consistently good advice

7. The judge determined that Arthur had made a **bona fide** contract with the roofing company.
   a. slipshod; invalid
   b. time-limited; temporary
   c. in good faith; genuine

Name: _____ Date: _____

FOREIGN WORDS AND PHRASES 2

If you don't already know these French words and phrases, you can learn them *tout de suite*!

Directions: Write a letter to match each **boldface** word or phrase with its meaning. Check a dictionary if you're not sure.

1. _____ We shouted "**Bon voyage**!" as the cruise ship departed.

2. _____ Meals ordered **a la carte** usually cost more.

3. _____ Samuel Clemens chose Mark Twain as his **nom de plume**.

4. _____ The wealthy woman expected service to be **tout de suite**.

5. _____ The seasoned politician was known for his **savoir faire**.

6. _____ Everyone admired the famous actress's amazing **couture**.

7. _____ To Mother Teresa, the poor were her **raison d´etre**.

8. _____ The U.S. Marine Corps is well known for its **esprit de corps**.

9. _____ Big spenders usually get **carte blanche** at Las Vegas hotels.

10. _____ The contractor built eight houses on the suburban **cul-de-sac**.

11. _____ Hoping for agreement, Francine asked, "**N´est-ce pas**?"

12. _____ My favorite **hors d´oeuvre** is caviar on toast points.

a. author's pen name

b. Is it not so?

c. group spirit

d. reason for existence

e. dead-end street

f. each food item separately priced

g. Have a good journey.

h. immediate

i. high-fashion clothing

j. social know-how

k. appetizer

l. freedom to do or have anything

Name: _____ Date: _____

SIMPLE IDIOMS 1

Every language has certain combinations of words that aren't meant to be taken literally. These phrases or expressions—called *idioms*—have special meanings. For example, to "hang out" at a certain place means to spend much of your time there.

A. Directions: Write a letter to match each **boldface** idiom on the left with its meaning on the right.

1. ____ to **talk out**   a. to answer disrespectfully
2. ____ to **talk back**   b. to be unwilling to go forward
3. ____ to **get by**   c. to rear from childhood
4. ____ to **hang back**   d. to pretend
5. ____ to **bring up**   e. to succeed or achieve a goal
6. ____ to **bring about**   f. to discuss at length
7. ____ to **make it**   g. to barely survive
8. ____ to **make believe**   h. to cause something to happen

B. Directions: Circle a letter to show the meaning of the **boldface** idiom.

1. Roland's name didn't **come up** in the conversation.
   a. wasn't mentioned   b. was put down   c. was flat

2. Some employees feared that the company would **go under**.
   a. be underground   b. go out of business   c. move to Australia

3. Rich didn't **come to** until two hours after his surgery.
   a. return to his room   b. move around   c. regain consciousness

4. I finished one exam, but I still have two **to go**.
   a. remaining   b. to take out   c. moving along

5. That new neighbor didn't **come across as** very likeable or friendly.
   a. walk toward me   b. seem to be   c. visit my house

Name: _____   Date: _____

SIMPLE IDIOMS 2

Directions: Circle the idiom that correctly completes each sentence.

1. Farhad (took down / **took up**) golf about two years ago.

2. Rita was (put on / **put off**) by Allie's bad attitude.

3. Mrs. Ha needed evidence to (**back up** / back down) her claim.

4. The team tried to (**pull off** / pull through) a trick play.

5. Joseph (ran down / **ran through**) his allowance very quickly.

6. If he ever needed help, Louis was certain that he could always (**fall back on** / fall in with) his family.

7. Right after Jan's husband died, she wasn't sure that she could (**carry on** / carry out).

8. Kenny was too busy to (take after / **take on**) another project.

9. Michele didn't (let out / **let on**) that she'd already heard the news.

10. On his way to work, Ben will (drop behind / **drop over**) for a visit.

INTERPRETING IDIOMS 1

Directions: Circle a letter to show the meaning of each **boldface** idiom.

1. Miguel's dance performance **brought down the house**.
   a. shook the stage
   b. was loudly applauded
   c. disappointed everyone

2. Miranda **looks down her nose** at all freshmen.
   a. feels much superior to
   b. is a lot taller than
   c. pays close attention to

3. The doting parents let their child **get away with murder**.
   a. ignore all rules
   b. kill people
   c. evade the police

4. Al tried very hard to **put two and two together**.
   a. introduce two couples
   b. multiply by 22
   c. sort out the facts

5. Derrick **runs rings around** all the other athletes.
   a. is much better than
   b. likes to run laps
   c. steals and sells rings

6. Sometimes it's a good idea to **let sleeping dogs lie**.
   a. try several solutions
   b. let problems solve themselves
   c. disturb the peace

7. Joanne was **knocked for a loop** by her mom's announcement.
   a. physically abused
   b. resentful of
   c. greatly surprised

8. Willie is **under the gun** to improve his grades.
   a. being pressured
   b. threatening others
   c. doing his best

Name: _____ Date: _____

INTERPRETING IDIOMS 2

Directions: Circle a letter to show the meaning of each **boldface** idiom.

1. Henry **took the bull by the horns** when he

   a. was attacked and gored.

   b. confronted his problem directly.

   c. overpowered a bigger opponent.

2. Why did Sherry try to **butter up** her teacher?

   a. to win favor with flattery

   b. to soften her skin

   c. to get a big laugh

3. Josh calls his job **a piece of cake** because

   a. he works in a bakery.

   b. he deserves a raise.

   c. it's very easy to do.

4. Shanika is **sitting pretty** right now because she's

   a. wearing lots of makeup.

   b. well-positioned for advancement.

   c. assigned to the best office.

5. When Ed shouted, **"Take a hike!"** he really meant

   a. "Stroll in the park!"

   b. "Leave right now!"

   c. "Get more exercise!"

6. By ordering her brother to **"Cut it out!"** Emily was telling him to

   a. remove her splinter.

   b. stop fooling around.

   c. finish his homework.

7. Someone who buys **a pig in a poke** can't

   a. afford the sales tax.

   b. see what is being purchased.

   c. get a bargain on pigs.

8. Why does Marvin say he **can't see the light at the end of the tunnel**?

   a. He feels discouraged and hopeless.

   b. He ignores the oncoming headlights.

   c. He has lost his eyesight.

EXPLAINING IDIOMS 1

Directions: Circle a letter to correctly answer each question.

What did you actually do if you . . .

1. **spilled the beans?**
   a. wasted food
   b. revealed a secret
   c. made a mess

2. **got wind of something?**
   a. smelled it
   b. heard about it
   c. imagined it

3. **hit the sack?**
   a. went to bed
   b. hit a punching bag
   c. struck out

4. **blew your own horn?**
   a. acted independently
   b. played a tune
   c. bragged about yourself

5. **threw in the towel?**
   a. washed yourself
   b. quit or gave up
   c. finished mopping

6. **got your back up?**
   a. started over
   b. became defensive
   c. displayed indifference

7. **let off steam?**
   a. expressed anger
   b. perspired heavily
   c. worked hard

8. **minded your p's and q's?**
   a. obeyed your parents
   b. cared for children
   c. were very careful

9. **pulled your own weight?**
   a. did your share
   b. did lots of chin-ups
   c. relied on others

10. **kept a straight face?**
    a. spoke pleasantly
    b. didn't smile or laugh
    c. had no wrinkles

Name: _____ Date: _____

EXPLAINING IDIOMS 2

A. Directions: Write the word that correctly completes each **boldface** idiom.

1. Daniel knew that his _____ was **cooked** when the teacher discovered his lie.

    chicken　　　pelican　　　goose　　　albatross

2. Someone who is **all** _____ should never become a surgeon.

    thumbs　　　shook up　　　ears　　　excited

3. Paul seemed to _____ **around the bush** instead of answering the question directly.

    run　　　twirl　　　dance　　　beat

4. Rosie and her friends like to _____ **the breeze** on their way home from school.

    enjoy　　　shoot　　　bat　　　taste

5. A clumsy guy like Roger is like a _____ **in a china shop**.

    bull　　　teacup　　　bully　　　watermelon

B. Directions: Draw a line to connect each idiom and its meaning.

People who are . . .

1. **breaking bread** are　　　　　　　　a. explaining in detail.

2. **talking shop** are　　　　　　　　　b. satisfying expectations.

3. **spelling it out** are　　　　　　　　c. sharing a meal.

4. **smelling the roses** are　　　　　　d. enjoying the day.

5. **cutting the mustard** are　　　　　e. discussing business.

USING IDIOMS IN CONTEXT 1

Use context clues to help you figure out the meaning of these commonly used idioms.

Directions: Circle a letter to complete each sentence with the correct idiom.

1. Someone with a great deal of energy and drive is often called a
   a. penny pincher.
   b. ball of fire.
   c. nervous Nellie.

2. If you want your brother to stop talking, you might tell him to
   a. button his lip.
   b. blow the whistle.
   c. eat a lemon.

3. Because Mrs. Smith is an excellent gardener, people say she
   a. turned over a new leaf.
   b. dishes dirt.
   c. has a green thumb.

4. Bill was bragging about his car when he claimed that it could
   a. jump in the lake.
   b. stop on a dime.
   c. eat up the miles.

5. By the time he retired, Dad said he was glad to
   a. leave the rat race.
   b. pay the piper.
   c. lend a hand.

6. When Jake wanted the waitress's attention, he tried to
   a. watch her back.
   b. grab her arm.
   c. catch her eye.

7. If you can't see any way out of a difficult situation, you feel that you are
   a. up a creek.
   b. around the bend.
   c. shooting the breeze.

8. You might ask a friend who's moving away to
   a. sing for his supper.
   b. drop you a line.
   c. go fly a kite.

Name: _____ Date: _____

USING IDIOMS IN CONTEXT 2

Directions: Select two appropriate idioms from the box to complete each sentence. Write the idioms on the lines.

pass the buck	talk out of both sides of her mouth	face the music
beat the rap	keep the wolf from the door	blowing his top
mend fences	threw the book at him	put much stock in
eat crow	bring home the bacon	give them the axe
in the bag	all in the same boat	

1. The criminal tried to _____, but the judge _____.

2. The employees were _____; every one of them was afraid the boss was about to _____.

3. After _____ at his sister, Brian cooled off and tried to _____.

4. At first Sandy tried to _____, but then she decided to admit her mistake and _____.

5. After boasting that their team's victory was _____, the fans had to _____ when their opponents won.

6. No one _____ the manager's promises because she was known to _____.

7. Her parents worked very hard to _____ and _____.

3-LETTER WORDS IN CONTEXT 1

Even very small words can add punch to your vocabulary. Following are a "gob" of three-letter words to add to your growing list.

Directions: Complete the sentences with words from the list. Hint: You will *not* use all the words. Check a dictionary if you need help.

| hex |
| spa |
| urn |
| pry |
| apt |
| nib |
| opt |
| irk |
| lea |
| sod |
| ebb |
| yen |
| eke |
| sue |

1. Another word for a bird's beak is _____.

2. Does it _____ you to wait in a long line to pay for your purchases?

3. Please put the cream and sugar next to the coffee _____.

4. Beginning actors are _____ to get nervous when they perform in front of strangers.

5. When there are few jobs available, it can be very hard to _____ out a living.

6. Their auto accident seemed to put a _____ on their cross-country trip.

7. At _____ tide, the water flows back to the sea.

8. Will our top student _____ to go to Harvard or to Yale?

9. The pregnant woman had a strong _____ for pickles and potato chips.

10. Dad used a crowbar to _____ open the wooden crate.

11. Laurie enjoys the sauna baths at the local health _____.

Name: _____ Date: _____

3-LETTER WORDS IN CONTEXT 2

Directions: Read the definitions of the three-letter words. Then use each word in an original sentence.

vie	to compete as a rival	**wit**	the ability to be clever
kin	relatives or family	**due**	expected at a certain time
ban	to forbid or prohibit	**wok**	metal cooking pan
sty	a pen for pigs	**wan**	having a pale, sickly color
woo	to try to win someone's love	**lax**	not strict, exact, or firm

1. _____

2. _____

3. _____

4. _____

5. _____

6. _____

7. _____

8. _____

9. _____

10. _____

Name: _____ **Date:** _____

4-LETTER WORDS IN CONTEXT 1

Now let's learn some four-letter words that could add some extra "dash" to your vocabulary!

Directions: Complete the sentences with words from the list. Hint: You will *not* use all the words. Check a dictionary if you need help.

Word List:
grim
idle
rout
fate
tuft
hare
skew
feat
vile
raze
shun
turf
cede
rite
trek
deem
abet
snub

1. The long _____ across the desert exhausted the travelers' water supply.

2. A demolition crew will be called in to _____ the old building.

3. The rifle company tried to _____ the enemy troops from their hideaway in the hills.

4. To _____ a criminal is to take part in the crime.

5. We found a _____ of bird feathers in the fallen nest.

6. Workers who often appear to be _____ won't keep their jobs for long.

7. Most people agree that _____ language is offensive and disgusting.

8. Why did Spain _____ Puerto Rico to the United States in 1898?

9. If you _____ alcohol and tobacco, you'll avoid many health problems.

10. Would you _____ it wise to take up skydiving?

11. A biased reporter may _____ the facts of a news story.

Name: _____ Date: _____

96 Building Vocabulary Skills and Strategies, Level 8 • Saddleback Publishing, Inc. ©2004 • 3 Watson, Irvine, CA 92618 • Phone (888) SDL-BACK • www.sdlback.com

4-LETTER WORDS IN CONTEXT 2

Directions: Read the definitions of the four-letter words. Then use each word in an original sentence.

avid	very eager or greedy	**gait**	way of walking or running
acme	the peak or highest point	**oust**	to get rid of
bias	partiality or prejudice	**pert**	lively, bold, saucy
site	the place where something is, was, or will be	**axis**	the straight line around which something turns
heed	to pay careful attention to	**rash**	too hasty or reckless

1. _____
2. _____
3. _____
4. _____
5. _____
6. _____
7. _____
8. _____
9. _____
10. _____

Name: _____ **Date:** _____

5-LETTER WORDS IN CONTEXT 1

Try adding some "verve" to your communication skills with some five-letter words. What is *verve*? It's energy and enthusiasm in the expression of ideas.

Directions: Complete the sentences with words from the list. Hint: You will *not* use all the words. Check a dictionary if you need help.

farce

tunic

elegy

debit

plush

acute

proxy

girth

allay

pithy

agile

sieve

1. Ancient Romans and Greeks wore a loose gown called a _____.

2. The _____ of a tree is determined by measuring around its trunk.

3. Their expensive hotel room was quite luxurious and _____.

4. To _____ her students' fears, the teacher stayed calm during the emergency.

5. A poem written in honor of someone who has recently died is called an _____.

6. An _____ medical problem must be treated immediately.

7. If you can't attend the session, you must cast your vote by _____.

8. His elaborate show of concern for us was clearly a _____.

9. A charge against your bank account is deducted as a _____.

10. The president's short speech was both powerful and _____.

Name: _____ Date: _____

5-LETTER WORDS IN CONTEXT 2

Directions: Read the words and their definitions. Then use each word in an original sentence.

deter	to prevent something from happening	**skulk**	to move about in a sneaky, threatening way
exile	to force someone to leave his or her own country	**orbit**	the path an object repeatedly follows around another object
seedy	shabby and untidy	**adept**	highly skilled; expert
dally	to waste time	**staid**	quiet, dignified, serious
tepid	slightly warm	**haven**	refuge; place of shelter

1. _____

2. _____

3. _____

4. _____

5. _____

6. _____

7. _____

8. _____

9. _____

10. _____

Name: _____ **Date:** _____

6-LETTER WORDS IN CONTEXT 1

Would you like to add some "polish" to your vocabulary? Try these six-letter words.

Directions: Circle the word that correctly completes the sentence. Check a dictionary if you need help.

1. A (pullet / pundit) is an expert who has great knowledge in a certain field.

2. That difficult puzzle will (baffle / banter) even a wordsmith like Ben.

3. You won't get to school on time if you (dabble / dawdle) along the way.

4. You (affirm / assign) the truth of something when you declare that it is so.

5. One candidate tried to (deform / defame) the other by making false statements about him.

6. A special (sensor / splice) in the camera measures the correct amount of light.

7. The robber had no (quaffs / qualms) about stealing the necklace.

8. The gracious innkeeper gave us a (hearty / hectic) welcome.

9. Mrs. Allen told her bored child not to (forage / fidget) in her seat.

10. The waiter poured hot coffee from a silver (chaise / carafe).

11. The (fiasco / finale) of the show featured a wonderful one-man band.

Name: _____ Date: _____

6-LETTER WORDS IN CONTEXT 2

Directions: Read the words and their definitions. Then use each word in an original sentence.

cavort	to romp, frolic, leap about playfully	**devise**	to work out, plan, or invent something
septic	causing infection	**berate**	to scold harshly
phobia	unreasonable fear of something	**status**	position, standing, or rank
innate	natural; inborn	**mentor**	one who advises or guides
exhort	to urge or strongly advise	**motive**	reason for doing something

1. _____

2. _____

3. _____

4. _____

5. _____

6. _____

7. _____

8. _____

9. _____

10. _____

Name: _____ Date: _____

7-LETTER WORDS IN CONTEXT 1

"Animate" your conversations with some of these challenging seven-letter words.

Directions: Complete each sentence with a word from the box. Hint: You will *not* use all the words. Check a dictionary if you need help.

catwalk	profane	platoon	bonanza	textile	fervent	carcass
terrain	oppress	tedious	gesture	geology	vintage	subsist

1. In a gold or silver mine, an especially rich deposit of ore is called a _____.

2. The hilly, rocky _____ made farming the land more difficult.

3. In good condition, a _____ automobile can be worth a lot of money.

4. There are many more soldiers in a company than there are in a _____.

5. A nod is a _____ that everyone understands.

6. Frontiersmen sometimes had to _____ on berries and wild game.

7. To hold people down by the cruel use of power is to _____ them.

8. The desperate earthquake victims made a _____ appeal for help.

9. Repeating the same tasks over and over again can be very _____.

10. _____ is the study of the Earth's crust and how its layers were formed.

11. A _____ mill produces knit or woven fabrics.

Name: _____ Date: _____

7-LETTER WORDS IN CONTEXT 2

Directions: Read the words and their definitions. Then use each word in an original sentence.

steeple high tower on a church or other building

prevail to be successful or win out

soprano highest singing voice of women or girls

hygiene the science that has to do with keeping healthy

servile excessive, slavelike humility

bizarre unbelievable; grotesque; very odd

skeptic one who questions things that most people believe

turmoil a noisy or confused condition

chagrin embarrassed feeling over one's own failure or disappointment

curator one in charge of a museum or library

1. _____
2. _____
3. _____
4. _____
5. _____
6. _____
7. _____
8. _____
9. _____
10. _____

Name: _____ Date: _____

8-LETTER WORDS IN CONTEXT 1

Speak with "vitality" and you will spread energy everywhere you go! Here are some eight-letter words to start you down the right road.

Directions: Complete the sentences with words from the list. Hint: You will *not* use all the words. Check a dictionary if you need help.

Word list:
- suffrage
- eligible
- latitude
- retrieve
- alliance
- monetary
- gingerly
- skirmish
- parallel
- genocide
- isolated
- efficacy
- virulent

1. Only students with a C average are _____ to play on the basketball team.

2. After the game, there was a brief _____ between fans of the opposing teams.

3. Brian felt _____ until he made some friends at his new school.

4. If you are concerned about _____ issues, you are worried about money.

5. Oak and Elm streets run _____ to one another.

6. Will you go and _____ our ball from the neighbor's backyard?

7. Bubonic plague is a _____ disease carried by infected rats.

8. The right to vote in political elections is called _____.

9. The Nazis committed _____ when they exterminated six million Jews.

10. Stated in degrees, _____ is the measurement of distance north or south of the equator.

11. A treaty that unites nations for some purpose is called an _____.

Name: _____ Date: _____

104 Building Vocabulary Skills and Strategies, Level 8 • Saddleback Publishing, Inc. ©2004 • 3 Watson, Irvine, CA 92618 • Phone (888) SDL-BACK • www.sdlback.com

8-LETTER WORDS IN CONTEXT 2

Directions: Read the words and their definitions. Then use each word in an original sentence.

colossal very great; enormous or immense

arrogant prideful, vain, haughty

conspire to plan together secretly

strategy a clever plan or scheme to manage or accomplish something

artifact something made by human work or skill, especially in the past

autonomy self-government; independence

souvenir a memento or keepsake

document a written record used to prove something

disclose to reveal or make known

instinct natural, inborn way of thinking or feeling

1. _____
2. _____
3. _____
4. _____
5. _____
6. _____
7. _____
8. _____
9. _____
10. _____

Name: _____ Date: _____

9-LETTER WORDS IN CONTEXT 1

An "expansive" vocabulary provides all the words you need to speak or write with confidence. Here are some nine-letter words to add to your list.

Directions: Complete the sentences with a word from the box. Hint: You will *not* use all the words. Check a dictionary if you need help.

| sophomore | repellent | improvise | outspoken | treachery | sculpture | dissuade |
| menagerie | migratory | tolerance | tradition | stalemate | mythology | ambitious |

1. To _____ is to quickly "make do" with whatever is at hand.

2. We show _____ when we're willing to accept that other people's beliefs are often different from our own.

3. A collection of wild animals kept in cages is called a _____.

4. An _____ person speaks frankly, even when it's not appropriate.

5. In her second year at college, Kayla is now a _____.

6. Thanksgiving dinner at my aunt's house has become a family _____.

7. An _____ fellow like Ty is always alert to opportunity.

8. Their argument couldn't be resolved; they had reached a _____.

9. George used an insect _____ to prevent mosquito bites.

10. _____ field workers travel from one job to another.

11. Melina's parents tried to _____ her from going into debt.

Name: _____   Date: _____

9-LETTER WORDS IN CONTEXT 2

Directions: Read the words and their definitions. Then use each word in an original sentence.

proponent one who proposes or supports a certain idea

redundant more than necessary; too much

reputable having a good reputation

pantomime use of gestures instead of words to tell a story

spectator one who watches something without taking part

symbolize to stand for or represent something

scoundrel villain, rascal, scallawag

exquisite beautiful; done with great care and skill

etiquette good manners; rules of proper behavior

speculate to think about something; contemplate; theorize

1. _____
2. _____
3. _____
4. _____
5. _____
6. _____
7. _____
8. _____
9. _____
10. _____

Name: _____ Date: _____

10-LETTER WORDS IN CONTEXT 1

Now you're on the road to becoming a "consummate" (highly skilled and accomplished) wordmaster! These 10-letter words will help you on your way.

Directions: Complete the sentences with a word from the box. Hint: You will *not* use all the words. Check a dictionary if you need help.

preference	vocational	lumberjack	evaluation	irrational
futuristic	resentment	pharmacist	unforeseen	fertilizer
efficiency	appreciate	indication	scandalous	immaturity

1. Lola's strong emotions caused her to make _____ decisions.

2. Preparing students for the workplace is the goal of _____ trainers.

3. After three months on the job, you will have your first performance _____.

4. The _____ has been busy filling prescriptions all afternoon.

5. _____ science fiction novels can give us a glimpse at what may actually happen someday.

6. Victor doesn't seem to _____ all the help he's been given.

7. We have many ice cream flavors; what is your _____?

8. _____ repair bills can wreck your budget.

9. Many people love to read _____ stories about the misdeeds of celebrities.

10. _____ is the art of competently performing tasks in a short amount of time.

11. The darkening clouds and strong winds were a clear _____ of an upcoming tornado.

Name: _____ Date: _____

10-LETTER WORDS IN CONTEXT 2

Directions: Read the words and their definitions. Then use each word in an original sentence.

boisterous rough; noisy; lively
comprehend to understand
affection fond, tender feeling; warm liking
incredible so unusual that it seems unbelievable
methodical done in an orderly, systematic way

particular specific; individual; not general
anticipate to expect or look forward to
conference a meeting held to discuss something
profession occupation requiring special education and training
eyewitness person who actually saw something happen

1. _____
2. _____
3. _____
4. _____
5. _____
6. _____
7. _____
8. _____
9. _____
10. _____

Name: _____ Date: _____

11-LETTER WORDS IN CONTEXT 1

A "diversified" stash of words allows you to speak out on *many different subjects.*

Directions: Complete the sentences with a word from the box. Hint: You will *not* use all the words. Check a dictionary if you need help.

partnership	dilapidated	consistency	overwhelmed	elimination
unblemished	monstrosity	documentary	spectacular	bittersweet
association	predictable	insensitive	destruction	information

1. The _____ old house had a gaping hole in the roof.

2. _____ of the slums was the goal of the downtown renewal project.

3. Given the long drought, reports of starvation had been sadly _____.

4. A successful _____ is usually based on mutual values and goals.

5. Critics call the huge new city hall a "glass and steel _____."

6. Her _____ memories of years gone by make her feel both happy and sad.

7. Everyone enjoyed the _____ fireworks display.

8. Did you see the TV _____ about the construction of the Brooklyn Bridge?

9. Mrs. Robinson often feels _____ by her heavy workload.

10. A truly considerate person is never _____ to other people's feelings.

11. The Chamber of Commerce is an _____ of local businesspeople.

Name: _____ Date: _____

11-LETTER WORDS IN CONTEXT 2

Directions: Read the words and their definitions. Then use each word in an original sentence.

participant one who takes part or shares in something

frustration being kept from doing or getting what you want

significant important; meaningful

investigate to search for facts; examine in detail

contraption strange-looking device that's hard to understand

subsequent coming after; later; following

concentrate to focus all one's thoughts or efforts

devastation total ruin or destruction

fundamental forming a basis or foundation; basic

convenience something that increases comfort or makes work less difficult

1. _____
2. _____
3. _____
4. _____
5. _____
6. _____
7. _____
8. _____
9. _____
10. _____

Name: _____ Date: _____

12-LETTER WORDS IN CONTEXT 1

The benefits of a good vocabulary are almost "unfathomable" (incapable of being understood or measured)!

Directions: Complete the sentences with words from the list. Hint: You will *not* use all the words. Check a dictionary if you need help.

Word list:
- postponement
- emancipation
- excruciating
- civilization
- coincidental
- announcement
- incompatible
- contribution
- anticipation
- constitution
- appendectomy
- condominium
- illustration
- relationship
- conservative
- manufacturer

1. The _____ between people and their pets has been studied for many years.
2. Hal has invented a new board game, and now he's looking for a _____.
3. Nuclear war could put an end to _____ as we know it.
4. Did you receive Tony and Tina's wedding _____ in the mail today?
5. The indefinite _____ of pay raises was bad news for the employees.
6. Anna hoped to sell 1,000 T-shirts, but her actual sales projection was cautiously _____.
7. The _____ Proclamation was signed by President Abraham Lincoln in 1862.
8. Before his emergency _____, the pain in Ronald's side was _____.
9. Roberto drew the beautiful _____ used on the cover of the yearbook.
10. Dan looked forward to the season's first track meet with great _____.
11. Our government's basic laws and rules are spelled out in the United States _____.

Name: _____ Date: _____

12-LETTER WORDS IN CONTEXT 2

Directions: Read the words and their definitions. Then use each word in an original sentence.

- **astronomical** having to do with astronomy; extremely great
- **humanitarian** doing good for others; helping humanity
- **intelligence** the ability to learn and understand
- **rehabilitate** to bring back to normal or good condition
- **apprehensive** fearful; hesitant
- **oceanography** science that studies the oceans and the animals and plants that live in them
- **experimental** based on a test or a trial; as yet unproven
- **discourteous** rude; impolite
- **regeneration** the act of being enlivened or renewed
- **afterthought** an idea that comes to mind later—perhaps too late

1. _____
2. _____
3. _____
4. _____
5. _____
6. _____
7. _____
8. _____
9. _____
10. _____

Name: _____ Date: _____

13-LETTER WORDS IN CONTEXT 1

These 13-letter words will help you become a "scintillating" (lively and sparkling) wordsmith.

Directions: Complete the sentences with words from the list. Hint: You will *not* use all the words. Check a dictionary if you need help.

Word list:
- uncomfortable
- environmental
- determination
- controversial
- irresponsible
- demonstration
- establishment
- predominantly
- international
- qualification
- revolutionary
- approximately
- justification
- comprehension
- monochromatic

1. _____ pollutants include waste products that have been dumped in rivers.
2. New leather shoes are often _____ until they've been worn a few times.
3. Politics and religion are two _____ subjects that are hotly debated.
4. If you don't have much help, it takes great _____ to achieve your goals.
5. The people in my neighborhood are _____ Central Americans.
6. There is no _____ for teasing a child until he cries.
7. Only an _____ babysitter would leave the house while the children are sleeping.
8. The newscast reported that _____ 100 people attended the city council meeting.
9. America's _____ War lasted from 1775 until 1783.
10. The salesperson will give you a _____ of how the new vacuum cleaner works.
11. The _____ of trade with other countries boosted the new nation's economy.

Name: _____ Date: _____

114 Building Vocabulary Skills and Strategies, Level 8

13-LETTER WORDS IN CONTEXT 2

Directions: Read the words and their definitions. Then use each word in an original sentence.

unconditional absolute; not subject to change

instantaneous in an instant or without delay

overconfident too sure of oneself

contamination the state of being dirty or impure

rearrangement a change in the previous order

questionnaire written list of questions used to gather information

sportsmanship the practice of good behavior and fair play in sport

perfectionist one who will not tolerate faults or errors

cosmetologist expert in the use of cosmetics

misconception a misunderstanding or wrong idea

1. _____
2. _____
3. _____
4. _____
5. _____
6. _____
7. _____
8. _____
9. _____
10. _____

Name: _____ Date: _____

JUST FOR FUN: EXPLAINING WHY OR WHY NOT

Words can be strange, fascinating, and amusing. You can have a bit of fun with these "Why or why not?" questions.

Directions: Check a dictionary to help you answer the questions.

1. Why would a **hippo** never be seen on a **hippodrome**?
   _____
   _____
   _____

2. Why is a **jowl** unable to dance a jig?
   _____
   _____
   _____

3. Why are you unlikely to see a **coati** in a coat closet?
   _____
   _____

4. Why might you find a **llama** on a **llano**?
   _____
   _____

5. Why would it amaze everyone to see a pony on a **pulpit**?
   _____
   _____

6. Why would it not be surprising to see a girl on a **gurney**?
   _____
   _____

7. Why are there never any **marmots** in the marketplace?
   _____
   _____

8. Why will **ozone** never become **obsolete**?
   _____
   _____

Name: _____   **Date:** _____

JUST FOR FUN: EXPLORING BIG WORDS

Big words can be *intimidating*. But don't let these monster words *scare* you. Have fun with them instead!

Directions: Check the dictionary definitions of the **boldface** words to help you answer the questions.

1. Who would be more likely to wait on you hand and foot—an **autocrat** or an **automaton**? Explain your thinking.
   _____
   _____
   _____
   _____

2. Is a hermit more likely to be a **misanthrope** or a **megalomaniac**? Explain your reasoning.
   _____
   _____

3. Would you rather be widely known as **pusillanimous** or **pulchritudinous**? Explain your answer.
   _____
   _____

4. If you live inland, would you probably eat more **vichyssoise** or **bouillabaisse**? Why?
   _____
   _____

5. What's the difference between a **troglodyte** and a **spelunker**? What do they have in common?
   _____
   _____

6. If you've been working very long hours, are you more likely to suffer from **lassitude** or **turpitude**? Why?
   _____
   _____

Name: _____ Date: _____

LITERATURE WORDS 1

Directions: Unscramble the words that match the definitions. Then use the unscrambled words to complete the crossword puzzle. Item 1-Across has been done for you.

ACROSS

1. _irony_ (ROYNI) — often humorous literary device; the opposite of what is expected
4. _____ (LOMBYS) — something that represents or stands for something else
6. _____ (ENTO) — the feeling given by the author's voice; attitude expressed by the author's language
10. _____ (CITFLONC) — the struggle between forces at the center of a story
12. _____ (AIDOGLUE) — words spoken by the characters in a novel or play
13. _____ (ODOM) — the overall feeling or atmosphere the author creates in a story
14. _____ (REACTRACH) — fictional person in a novel or story
15. _____ (HEMET) — the central meaning; the main idea of a story
16. _____ (EVONL) — long form of fictional literature with a complex plot
17. _____ (TOLP) — the chain of events in a story that leads to its outcome
18. _____ (LORAM) — the lesson to be drawn by the reader

DOWN

2. _____ (NOTIRLOUSE) — the conclusion or outcome of a story's struggle or conflict
3. _____ (EGSTINT) — the time and place a story takes place
4. _____ (ELYST) — the author's special use of language to express experience and literary form
5. _____ (XCLAIM) — the outcome of a story's main conflict
7. _____ (TARNROAR) — the character who tells the story in his or her own words
8. _____ (NOICTIF) — literary work in which the plot and characters come from the author's imagination
9. _____ (THUROA) — the writer of a story, novel, etc.
11. _____ (COVIE) — combination of the author's personality and unique literary tools

LITERATURE WORDS 2

Directions: Use the crossword puzzle answers to correctly complete the sentences.

1. The _____ between man and the weather is at the center of many sea stories.

2. Stephen King is a very successful American _____.

3. The _____ of an O. Henry short story is almost always a surprise ending.

4. Every one of Aesop's famous fables embodies a _____ lesson.

5. *Brave New World* is Aldous Huxley's most famous _____.

6. To maintain the reader's interest, a mystery story must have a fast-moving _____.

7. The _____ of the novel *Cold Mountain* is the South during America's Civil War.

8. In all of world literature, Shakespeare's _____ is unique.

9. A character named Ishmael is the _____ of *Moby Dick*.

10. Captain Ahab is the main _____ in *Moby Dick*.

11. Neil Simon's skill at writing clever _____ makes his plays very popular.

12. The letter *A* is an important _____ in Nathaniel Hawthorne's novel, *The Scarlet Letter*.

Name: _____ Date: _____

HUMAN BODY WORDS 1

Directions: Unscramble the words that match the definitions. Then use the unscrambled words to complete the crossword puzzle. Item 2-Across has been done for you.

ACROSS

2. __embryo__ (ROBYEM) — offspring in the first stages of its growth, while still in the uterus
3. _____ (STATENOIG) — the period of time an offspring develops in the mother before birth
7. _____ (NORMSHOE) — substances produced by glands and then circulated in the blood
9. _____ (MESSOMOORCH) — threadlike parts of a cell's nucleus made up of DNA and genes
12. _____ (ESNIP) — the backbone
13. _____ (EXFLER) — a muscle's automatic reaction to nerve stimulation
14. _____ (RYERAT) — blood vessel that carries blood away from the heart
15. _____ (SNEEG) — parts of chromosomes that control the development of individual traits
16. _____ (MAYNOAT) — the study of the form or structure of animals or plants
17. _____ (SNIVE) — blood vessels that carry blood back to the heart from some part of the body

DOWN

1. _____ (REMUF) — the big bone in the upper part of the leg
4. _____ (OTARA) — the main artery of the body
5. _____ (SPECIB) — the large muscle in the front of the upper arm
6. _____ (RATHE) — the hollow muscle in the chest that pumps blood to the arteries through the veins
7. _____ (THERYDIE) — the passing of traits from parents to offspring
8. _____ (GROANS) — parts of the body, like heart and lungs, that have some special purpose
10. _____ (NESESS) — the powers of sight, hearing, touch, taste, and smell
11. _____ (RINAB) — the organ in the skull that controls many of the body's processes

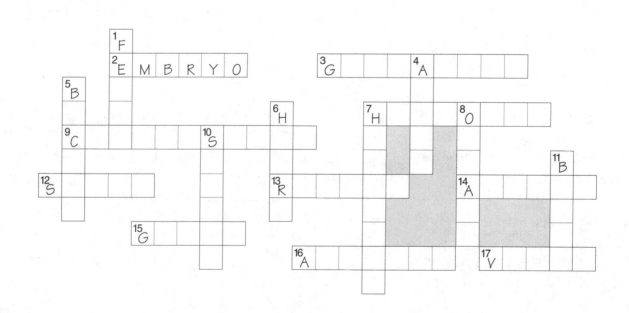

HUMAN BODY WORDS 2

Directions: Use the crossword puzzle answers to correctly complete the sentences.

1. The human _____ is the center of thought, memory, and emotion.

2. Messages go downward from your brain to a long rope of neurons in your _____.

3. If you want to name every part of the human body, you should take an _____ class.

4. A human baby has a _____ period of nine months.

5. The thighbone, or _____, is the largest bone in the body.

6. The heart, arteries, and veins are the _____ of your circulatory system.

7. During puberty, certain glands in the body begin to produce _____.

8. Every trait you inherit, such as eye color, is controlled by at least one pair of _____.

9. The color of your hair is determined by _____.

10. _____ are tiny particles in the nucleus of cells that pass on inherited characteristics.

11. When you "make a muscle," the _____ in your upper arm bulges.

GEOGRAPHY WORDS 1

Directions: Unscramble the words that match the definitions. Then use the unscrambled words to complete the crossword puzzle. Item 1-Across has been done for you.

ACROSS

1. _strait_ (ATRITS) — narrow body of water joining two larger ones
6. _____ (LATED) — triangle of land formed from soil deposited at the mouth of a large river
7. _____ (ERFE) — ridge of sand, coral, or rock lying near the surface of the water
9. _____ (CATCIR) — region around the North Pole
11. _____ (SHIMEREEPH) — any half into which the earth's surface has been divided in geography
13. _____ (SORENOI) — slow wearing away of soil by wind and water
14. _____ (SEAM) — large, high rock having steep sides and a flat top
16. _____ (FLUG) — large area of ocean reaching into land
17. _____ (SNABI) — all the land drained by a river and its branches
18. _____ (ONONMOS) — a wind of the Indian Ocean and southern Asia

DOWN

1. _____ (VASNANA) — flat, open region with bunches of stiff grass; a plain
2. _____ (SHMITSU) — a narrow strip of land joining two larger areas of land
3. _____ (NIPEALSUN) — long piece of land almost completely surrounded by water
4. _____ (EPSPET) — extensive treeless plain in Europe or Asia, often grass-covered and semiarid
5. _____ (CLEARIG) — huge mass of ice and snow that moves slowly down a mountain or across land
8. _____ (NIMAFE) — human starvation throughout a wide region because of lack of food
10. _____ (SCRIPTO) — hot region of the earth between the Tropic of Capricorn and the Tropic of Cancer
12. _____ (RIOVERSER) — place where water is collected and stored for later use
15. _____ (NEGJUL) — tropical land covered with thick trees, filled with animals that prey on each other

GEOGRAPHY WORDS 2

Directions: Use the crossword puzzle answers to correctly complete the sentences.

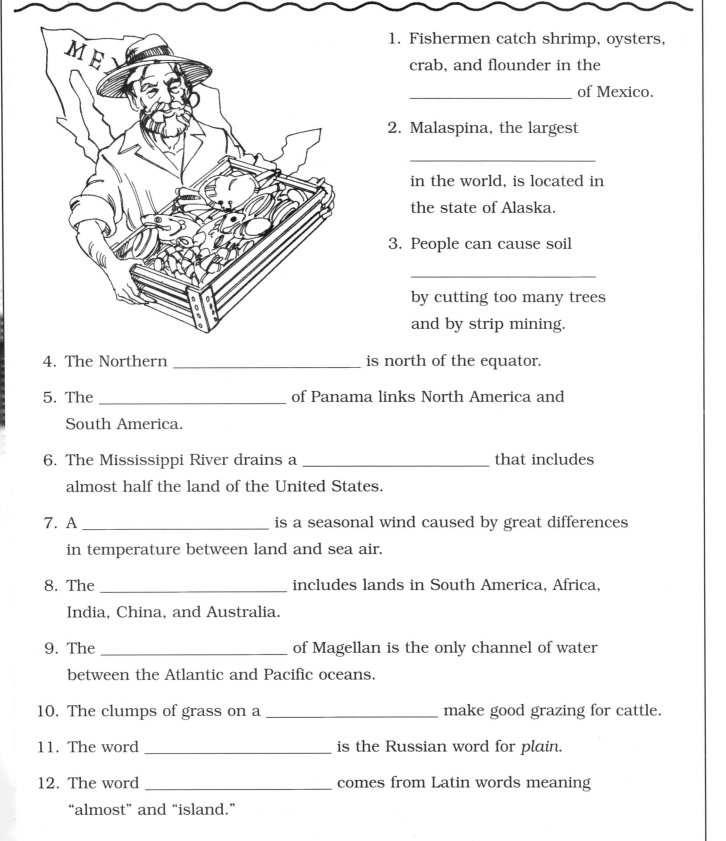

1. Fishermen catch shrimp, oysters, crab, and flounder in the _____ of Mexico.

2. Malaspina, the largest _____ in the world, is located in the state of Alaska.

3. People can cause soil _____ by cutting too many trees and by strip mining.

4. The Northern _____ is north of the equator.

5. The _____ of Panama links North America and South America.

6. The Mississippi River drains a _____ that includes almost half the land of the United States.

7. A _____ is a seasonal wind caused by great differences in temperature between land and sea air.

8. The _____ includes lands in South America, Africa, India, China, and Australia.

9. The _____ of Magellan is the only channel of water between the Atlantic and Pacific oceans.

10. The clumps of grass on a _____ make good grazing for cattle.

11. The word _____ is the Russian word for *plain*.

12. The word _____ comes from Latin words meaning "almost" and "island."

EARTH SCIENCE WORDS 1

Directions: Unscramble the words that match the definitions. Then use the unscrambled words to complete the crossword puzzle. Item 2-Across has been done for you.

ACROSS

2. _conservation_ (SNOCREVNOITA) the wise and careful use of our natural resources
5. _____ (PYTOHON) a stormy tropical cyclone over the Pacific Ocean
7. _____ (TAMICLE) the average weather in a region over many years
9. _____ (LISFOS) remains of a long-dead organism embedded in the earth's crust
12. _____ (TENORNIVMEN) all the things that surround anything
13. _____ (OCRE) the center of the earth
14. _____ (SMOTAPHREE) all the air around the earth
16. _____ (ROSTAMYON) the science that studies the size, makeup, and motion of stars, planets, etc.
17. _____ (YAXLAG) any vast group of stars such as the Milky Way
18. _____ (NEDNOCSONAIT) the process by which a gas turns into a liquid

DOWN

1. _____ (BITOR) path followed by an object in space as it repeatedly goes around another
2. _____ (STENNOTNIC) the seven major land masses of planet Earth
3. _____ (RAE) period of history; one of five main divisions of time in geology
4. _____ (ESPLIEC) darkening of the sun when the moon passes between the sun and the earth
6. _____ (NAPSELT) large celestial bodies that revolve around the sun
8. _____ (GOYLOGE) the study of the earth's crust including its rocks and fossils
10. _____ (NOEZO) a form of oxygen in a thin layer within the stratosphere
11. _____ (EROTME) a rocky fragment from space that burns when it enters Earth's atmosphere
13. _____ (STRUC) the thin outer layer of the earth
15. _____ (ASNOCE) huge bodies of saltwater covering more than two-thirds of the earth's surface

EARTH SCIENCE WORDS 2

Directions: Use the crossword puzzle answers to correctly complete the sentences.

1. The seven _____ are Africa, Asia, Australia, Antarctica, North America, South America, and Europe.

2. Earth's _____ are named the Atlantic, the Pacific, the Indian, and the Arctic.

3. The continents and the ocean floors are part of Earth's _____.

4. In their order from the sun, the _____ are Mercury, Venus, Earth, Mars, Jupiter, Saturn, Uranus, Neptune, and Pluto.

5. Dinosaurs flourished during the Mesozoic _____, which became known as the "age of reptiles."

6. When you see dew on the grass, you are looking at an example of _____.

7. The three main types of _____ are tropical, polar, and temperate.

8. A _____ that makes a bright streak of light as it burns is often called a "shooting star."

9. Scientists think the _____ of the earth is probably made of nickel and iron.

10. Experts in _____ measure radioactivity to determine the age of rocks.

11. A _____ is a group of stars, dust, and gases held together by gravitational force.

Name: _____ Date: _____

PHYSICAL SCIENCE WORDS 1

Directions: Unscramble the words that match the definitions. Then use the unscrambled words to complete the crossword puzzle. Item 1-Across has been done for you.

ACROSS

1. __battery__ (RYBTATE) — a device that changes chemical energy into electrical energy
5. _____ (STEMELEN) — the basic substances of which all matter is made
7. _____ (AMNICHE) — a device designed to change the speed, direction, or amount of a force
8. _____ (ROPESTRIPE) — qualities of matter such as color, shape, odor, and hardness
10. _____ (ROFEC) — any push or pull on an object
12. _____ (TYVGAIR) — the force of attraction between any two objects that have mass
14. _____ (IDQUIL) — matter with a definite volume but no definite shape
16. _____ (STOMA) — microscopic parts into which all things on earth can be broken down
17. _____ (CEPMURTS) — the rainbowlike band of color seen when white light is refracted
18. _____ (TISCHEMRY) — the scientific study of substances and how they change when combined with other substances
19. _____ (TAGNEM) — a stone or piece of metal that attracts iron or steel

DOWN

2. _____ (NOOLGYCHET) — the application of scientific and industrial skills to practical use
3. _____ (MERATT) — everything, living or nonliving, that takes up space
4. _____ (DOLIS) — matter with a definite shape and volume
6. _____ (ERENYG) — the power of certain forces in nature to do work
9. _____ (SCISYPH) — the scientific study of energy and how it interacts with matter
10. _____ (TOCRIFIN) — the force that slows down the motion of moving objects or surfaces that touch
11. _____ (MIRSP) — a glass, triangular-shaped object that can separate a ray of white light into the colors of the rainbow
13. _____ (AUCVUM) — the absence of matter
15. _____ (SAG) — matter with neither a definite shape nor a definite volume

PHYSICAL SCIENCE WORDS 2

Directions: Use the crossword puzzle answers to correctly complete the sentences.

1. Contact with the sidewalk causes _____, which slows down the rolling motion of a skateboard's wheels.

2. Oxygen, nitrogen, gold, and silver are examples of the 103 known _____.

3. The steam created by a hot shower is an example of a _____.

4. The _____ in a flashlight is made of two different kinds of metal and some kind of acid.

5. A common crowbar is a good example of a simple _____.

6. When you see a bolt of lightning, you are looking at an example of electrical _____.

7. _____ pulls all matter toward the center of the earth.

8. Solids, liquids, and gases are different states of _____.

9. The colors in the _____ are red, orange, yellow, green, blue, indigo, and violet.

10. Copper and lead both occur in nature as _____ elements.

11. You may use a _____ to stick photos or notes on your refrigerator.

12. Advances in _____ have enabled doctors to develop many lifesaving medical treatments.

Name: _____ Date: _____

AMERICAN HISTORY WORDS 1

Directions: Unscramble the words that match the definitions. Then use the unscrambled words to complete the crossword puzzle. Item 2-Across has been done for you.

ACROSS

2. _ancestors_ (SECANSORT) those who have lived before us in a family line; forefathers
3. _____ (REPBLAME) the beginning part of a document, such as a constitution
9. _____ (RIONEEPS) those people who go somewhere first, to open the way for others
11. _____ (AXT) money paid by citizens to support a government
12. _____ (SOOLNICE) lands settled and ruled by people from other countries
15. _____ (OSDQUARTSCION) Spanish conquerors of other lands
16. _____ (ILOVENURTO) the overthrow of a government, with another taking its place
18. _____ (CODNITER) an important set of beliefs or principles
19. _____ (RUBSBUR) districts where people live on the outskirts of a city
20. _____ (AILIMIT) local groups of citizens who act as soldiers but have little military training

DOWN

1. _____ (TRAIPSTO) American colonists who wanted independence from England
4. _____ (BOILNATIO) the official act of forbidding slavery
5. _____ (FLUBOFA) another name for the North American bison, a wild kind of ox
6. _____ (AIRSRIPE) large areas of flat or rolling grasslands
7. _____ (NORETRIF) the outer limit of settled country next to untamed wilderness
8. _____ (CARCOMEDY) government in which the people hold the ruling power
10. _____ (MISTRANGIM) people who come to a foreign country to make a new home
13. _____ (CEMOONY) a country's system of producing, distributing, and consuming wealth
14. _____ (ROTSTEP) the people's right to speak out against government policy
17. _____ (BLEER) nickname for a Confederate soldier in the American Civil War

AMERICAN HISTORY WORDS 2

Directions: Use the crossword puzzle answers to correctly complete the sentences.

1. Riding in covered wagons, the _____ crossed the vast _____ on their way west.

2. Railroad companies saw the vast herds of _____ as a cheap source of food for their workers.

3. Patrick Henry, Paul Revere, and Thomas Paine are remembered as great American _____.

4. The American _____ began in 1775 and ended in 1783.

5. More than 35 million _____ entered the United States between 1840 and 1920.

6. Hernando Cortes and Francisco Pizarro were _____ who claimed new lands in the name of Spain.

7. America's 13 original _____ were settled by people from England, Holland, and other European countries.

8. _____ of slavery was finally achieved by the Emancipation Proclamation in 1863.

9. In 1823, the Monroe _____ warned Europe not to start new American colonies or try to reclaim old ones.

10. The Boston Tea Party was a _____ against an unfair _____ on the colonists.

11. When American towns were attacked by the British, local men formed a _____ to fight back.

Name: _____ Date: _____

WORLD HISTORY WORDS 1

Directions: Unscramble the words that match the definitions. Then use the unscrambled words to complete the crossword puzzle. Item 3-Across has been done for you.

ACROSS

3. **Holocaust** (THUSACOOL) — the killing of millions of Jews by German Nazis
6. _____ (CRUTE) — an agreement between enemies to stop fighting
9. _____ (HOPRAHA) — a king of ancient Egypt
10. _____ (VALIDEEM) — belonging to the Middle Ages, about A.D. 500 to A.D. 1450
12. _____ (TRYATE) — an agreement, usually having to do with peace or trade
13. _____ (DEATHPAIR) — the official separation of races, based mainly on skin color
15. _____ (BRISEC) — in ancient times, one who wrote out copies of contracts
16. _____ (MYMMU) — body preserved with chemicals by ancient Egyptians
17. _____ (INVICATZILOI) — the society and culture of a particular people, place, or period
18. _____ (STIGCHARLOOE) — scientist who studies past cultures by digging up the remains of ancient towns

DOWN

1. _____ (SPHERSOILHOP) — scholars who study such things as the meaning of life, right and wrong, etc.
2. _____ (GOAT) — loose outer garment worn by patricians in ancient Rome
4. _____ (FRESS) — people legally tied to the land; farm workers much like slaves
5. _____ (SONDAM) — people who move from place to place in search of food, water, and grazing land
7. _____ (STEACS) — the social classes into which the people of India are divided
8. _____ (STROIGMACP) — early writing using pictures instead of letters or symbols
9. _____ (GLUEAP) — a deadly disease that spreads quickly
11. _____ (CUPRIBLE) — government in which citizens have the right to elect representatives to make law
14. _____ (RIPEME) — a group of lands under the control of one government or ruler

WORLD HISTORY WORDS 2

Directions: Use the crossword puzzle answers to correctly complete the sentences.

1. The ancient Egyptians called their ruler _____, meaning "the great house."

2. In _____ times, _____ were forbidden to leave the land on which they were born.

3. Socrates, Plato, and Aristotle were the most famous of the brilliant Greek _____.

4. A wealthy landowner in ancient Rome wore a _____ to show his importance.

5. The peace _____ ending World War I was signed in 1919.

6. In the Middle Ages, several outbreaks of bubonic _____ killed millions of Europeans.

7. Tribes of _____ were called "barbarians" by the citizens of the Roman Empire.

8. In the Roman _____, 300 elected representatives met in a senate.

9. The _____ was what Adolph Hitler called the "final solution of the Jewish problem."

10. Ancient Egyptian _____ was centered around the Nile River Valley.

11. In South Africa, _____ was not officially ended until 1992.

12. As early as 3500 B.C. the Sumerians began using _____ to keep records.

Name: _____ Date: _____

ART WORDS 1

Directions: Unscramble the words that match the definitions. Then use the unscrambled words to complete the crossword puzzle. Item 1-Across has been done for you.

ACROSS

1. _perspective_ (REPSTECVIPE) — the art of picturing things to make them seem close or far away, big or small, etc.
5. _____ (RETAWSOLORC) — paints made by mixing coloring matter with water instead of oil
12. _____ (TECKSH) — a simple drawing, usually done quickly and with little detail
14. _____ (SANDLPACE) — a picture of outdoor scenery that can be seen in one view
16. _____ (STAIRT) — one who works in any of the fine arts, especially painting, drawing, etc.
17. _____ (SILO) — paints made by mixing coloring matter with oil
18. _____ (SCORFE) — the art of painting with watercolors on wet plaster
19. _____ (TALPTEE) — thin board with a hole for the thumb at one end, used by an artist for mixing paints
20. _____ (GLYREAL) — room or building for showing or selling works of art

DOWN

2. _____ (YALC) — a sticky earth material used by sculptors to model a figure
3. _____ (TROPAIRT) — drawing, painting, photograph, etc. of a person, especially of the face
4. _____ (PLUSCURTE) — the art of shaping stone, metal, or other materials into statues or figures
6. _____ (CETH) — to engrave a drawing or design by using acid on a metal or glass surface
7. _____ (SUMMUE) — building or room for displaying important art, history, or science objects
8. _____ (GIDNES) — the artistic arrangement of parts, colors, etc. to have a certain effect
9. _____ (DOMEL) — a person who poses for an artist or photographer
10. _____ (RACHLOAC) — a form of carbon used as pencils, sticks, etc. for drawing
11. _____ (BRALEM) — hard limestone, sometimes streaked, used as a building material for statues
13. _____ (SLEEA) — a standing frame for holding an artist's canvas, a picture, etc.
15. _____ (SAVNAC) — heavy cotton or linen cloth stretched on a frame to be used for oil painting

ART WORDS 2

Directions: Use the crossword puzzle answers to correctly complete the sentences.

1. Rodin's most famous _____ is of a man he called "The Thinker."

2. Satisfied with her final pencil _____, Annmarie was ready to start painting.

3. The artwork at that uptown _____ costs a lot more than we can afford.

4. The Louvre is a famous art _____ in Paris, France.

5. The artist mixed blue and yellow on his _____ to make the shade of green he wanted.

6. Gabriel placed his _____ by a window so he could paint in natural light.

7. Artists often use _____ to paint delicate subjects, such as pink and white flowers.

8. Rembrandt used _____ to paint his much-admired artworks.

9. Gilbert Stuart's _____ of George Washington is the best-known image of our first president.

10. Michelangelo's huge statue of David is 18 feet high and made of solid _____.

11. The great Renaissance _____ Leonardo da Vinci was also a brilliant scientist.

Name: _____ Date: _____

ESSAY TEST WORDS 1

Directions: Unscramble the words that match the definitions. Then use the unscrambled words to complete the crossword puzzle. Item 4-Across has been done for you.

ACROSS

4. _paraphrase_ (HAPRASPARE) — to restate something written or spoken; to express something in different words
8. _____ (FECTEF) — anything that is caused by something else; a result
12. _____ (TROMELAUF) — to put into words in a clear and exact way
13. _____ (YUJSIFT) — to give reasons why something is right or fair
14. _____ (ZIERAMSUM) — to briefly restate the main points of something
15. _____ (REPINTERT) — to explain the meaning of something in your own words
16. _____ (LAYNEAZ) — to carefully examine something by separating it into its parts
17. _____ (TEAMISTE) — to make a general but careful guess about the cost, size, quality, or value of something

DOWN

1. _____ (NARK) — to position people or things in order, as measured by quality or importance
2. _____ (CRATE) — to show the trail leading to something; to track its development
3. _____ (ENLARGE) — having to do with the main parts, but not with details; not specialized or specific
5. _____ (CESYPIF) — to tell in detail; to mention definitely and specifically
6. _____ (ETIC) — to name or quote from something
7. _____ (SCUDSIS) — to give opinions and ideas about something in speech or writing
9. _____ (INLOUTE) — to set out the main points of something from beginning to end
10. _____ (CIDTREP) — to tell what one thinks will happen in the future; to forecast
11. _____ (TREALE) — to tell about or give an account of something

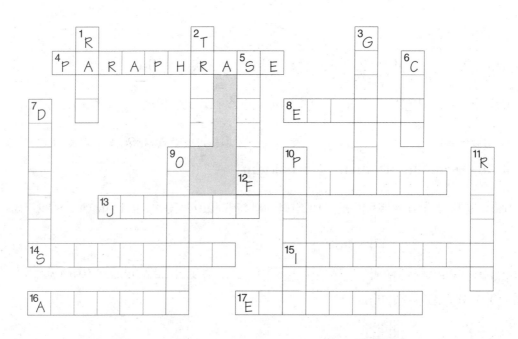

ESSAY TEST WORDS 2

Directions: Use the crossword puzzle answers to correctly complete the sentences.

1. The scientist will _____ the fossil to determine its approximate age.

2. To _____ a controversial issue, mention both the pros and cons of the argument.

3. _____ the circumstances and events that led to the outbreak of World War I.

4. Giving reasons for your opinions, _____ the top three U.S. presidents of the 20th century.

5. What was the immediate _____ of the bombing of Pearl Harbor?

6. It was difficult for the generals to _____ just how long the war would last.

7. _____ the meaning of Julius Caesar's statement, "Veni, vidi, vici."

8. If you use a direct quote from a speech, be sure to _____ the speaker.

9. We were asked to _____ the plot of Romeo and Juliet in three short paragraphs.

10. Roman numerals are often used to identify the major headings in an _____.

11. Past events do not always help us to _____ what will occur in the future.

SCOPE & SEQUENCE

STUDENT	FORMAL/INFORMAL LANGUAGE	ALPHABETICAL ORDER	DENOTATION	CONNOTATION	EUPHEMISMS/DYSPHEMISMS	VARIANT VOWEL SOUNDS	SILENT LETTERS	SYLLABICATION	ACCENT MARKS	CONTEXT CLUES	VARIANT WORD FORMS	COMPOUND WORDS	GREEK ROOTS	LATIN ROOTS	PREFIXES	SUFFIXES	NEAR MISSES	SYNONYMS: NOUNS	SYNONYMS: VERBS	SYNONYMS: ADJECTIVES

SCOPE & SEQUENCE

STUDENT	SYNONYMS: ADVERBS	ANTONYMS: NOUNS	ANTONYMS: VERBS	ANTONYMS: ADJECTIVES	ANTONYMS: ADVERBS	HOMOPHONES	HOMOGRAPHS	ACRONYMS	CLIPPED WORDS	SIMPLE IDIOMS	IDIOMS IN CONTEXT	LITERATURE WORDS	HUMAN BODY WORDS	GEOGRAPHY WORDS	EARTH SCIENCE WORDS	PHYSICAL SCIENCE WORDS	AMERICAN HISTORY WORDS	WORLD HISTORY WORDS	ART WORDS	ESSAY TEST WORDS

ANSWER KEY

PAGE 6
A. 1. inquire
2. fatigued
3. residence
4. eschew
5. incensed
6. converse
7. heinous
8. procure
9. petulant
10. encounter
B. 1. c 3. a 5. b
2. a 4. c

PAGE 7
A. 1. hitched
2. nuthouse
3. dude
4. spiffy
5. creamed
6. busted
B. 1. chummy
2. talkative
3. eccentric
4. egghead
5. tattle
6. harass

PAGE 8
A. 1. neutral 3. first
2. third 4. quickly
B. 1. capacity
2. condemn
3. congratulations
4. excursion
5. exemption
6. gird
7. gravitate
8. italic
9. jargon
10. latitude
11. lithe
12. lustrous
13. nymph
14. opaque
15. optic
16. phylum
17. purport
18. rigor
19. roster
20. thesis
21. victorious

PAGE 9
A. 1. Cross out: falter, flit, flout
2. Answers will vary. Some possible answers: flatfoot, flatter, flaw, flax, flay, fleece
B. 1. between 3. will
2. back 4. after
C. Circle: pepsin, percale, pepperoni
Circle: devious, dewlap, diabetes, diabolic

PAGE 10
A. 1. bullies 4. lice
2. echoes 5. alumni
3. solos 6. children
B. 1. rise 3. beginning
2. said 4. think
C. 1. most beautiful
2. gorier
3. most
4. more serious

PAGE 11
A. 1. moustache
2. fulfil
3. jeweler
4. quintet
5. cacti
6. cagey
7. cocoanut
8. abridgement
B. 1. c 3. e 5. f 7. g
2. d 4. a 6. b

PAGE 12
A. 1. N 4. N 7. P 10. N
2. P 5. N 8. N 11. N
3. P 6. P 9. N 12. P
B. 1. stalk
2. squander
3. fascinated
4. alibi
5. cunning
6. conspicuous
7. struggle
8. investigate
9. distort
10. villain

PAGE 13
1. scrawny
2. food
3. terminate
4. runty
5. die
6. observe
7. jailbird
8. economical
9. frivolous
10. visitor
11. grind
12. inquisitive
13. eat

PAGE 14
Approximate answers:
1. The words sorrel, piebald, and roan are colors of horses (equine animals), not pigs (porcine animals).
2. Karoo is a plateau in South Africa. Karnak is a village in Egypt.
3. Since turpitude is wickedness, you'd be more likely to be praised for your rectitude, or good moral character.
4. No. It wouldn't make sense to put salad dressing on a bowl of fish soup.
5. A virtuoso is an expert at the fine arts, especially music. If a performing musician made a mistake, his cheeks might be bright red (vermilion) with embarrassment.
6. A satirist, who uses wit to make fun of humankind, would make the best comedian. A somnambulist is a sleepwalker.
7. You might tame a ferret, which is a polecat. A garret is an attic room. A turret is a dome containing a gun.

PAGE 15
Approximate answers:
1. A troglodyte is a cave dweller; bats live in caves.
2. On a tombstone. It might say, "He loved good food."
3. In Italy. You'd be outdoors.
4. Yes. Polygamy means having many spouses. Polyandrists have many husbands, and polygynists have many wives.
5. You'd hire a prestidigitator, which is a magician. A mountebank is a deceiver—often a fake healer.
6. As a bad-tempered person, a curmudgeon would likely be curt.
7. Both were Native American tribes. The Kansa lived in Kansas, and the Karok lived in northwestern California.

PAGE 16
A SOUNDS
1. animal, happen
2. rayon, explain
3. walnut, altar
4. daring, scarce
5. party, scar
6. senator, agree
E SOUNDS
1. next, edge
2. legal, maybe
3. some, place
4. shower, operate
5. agent, often
I SOUNDS
1. different, little
2. giant, spider
3. circus, affirm

O SOUNDS
1. problem, opera
2. poem, ocean
3. towel, hour
4. loyal, void
5. coffee, along
6. wooden, wool
7. tool, smooth
8. weapon, obstruct

PAGE 17
A. **U SOUNDS**
1. hundred, uncle
2. pupil, future
3. bullfrog, ambush
4. duty, solution
5. occur, urgent
B. 1. where 6. although
2. hay 7. hooray
3. noun 8. crude
4. hassle 9. slate
5. seed 10. endow

PAGE 18
A. SILENT LETTER | CROSS OUT
1. c reject, fraction
2. w shower, wash
3. t rafter, lofty
4. l album, enamel
5. g logic, twig
6. b number, tremble
7. s moist, fashion
8. k monkey, oak
9. n hymnal, snare
10. p lumpy, respond
B. 1. autumn 3. adjective
2. knuckle 4. knife

PAGE 19
A. 1. Fasten 4. knead
2. gnaw 5. kneel
3. Psalms 6. Rhapsody
B. ACROSS: 3. scene
5. rhyme 7. gnat
8. knit
DOWN: 1. gnome
2. rhythm 3. scent
4. write 6. knock

PAGE 20
A. 1. **2-SYLLABLE WORDS**
slug´•gish
con´•jure
stat´•ic
ger´•bil
2. **3-SYLLABLE WORDS**
cha•ris´•ma
in•sur´•ance
la´•bor•er
dig´•it•al
3. **4-SYLLABLE WORDS**
pre•mo•ni´•tion
ad´•ver•sar•y
ex•or´•bi•tant
ger•an´•i•um

4. 5-SYLLABLE WORDS
   si • mul • ta´• ne • ous
   chor • e • og´• ra • phy
   in • con • spic´• u • ous
   mel • o • dra • mat´• ic
B. 1. LA • bor • er
   2. cha • RIS • ma
   3. ex • OR • bi • tant
   4. mel • o • dra • MAT • ic

PAGE 21
A. 1. second   5. second
   2. first   6. third
   3. first   7. first
   4. second   8. first
B. 1. min´• ute (noun)
      min • ute´ (adjective)
   2. re • cord´ (verb)
      re´• cord (noun)
   3. des´• ert (noun)
      des • ert´ (verb)
   4. pres • ent´ (verb)
      pres´• ent (noun)

PAGE 22
ANSWER   CIRCLE WORD
1. c   shoaty
2. a   bromps
3. c   revmoc
4. b   dibble
5. c   murty
6. a   krinks
7. b   sprictic
8. a   wakruk

PAGE 23
1. b   3. a   5. c
2. c   4. b   6. b

PAGE 24
1. symbol   6. customers
2. concept   7. journal
3. assistant   8. medal
4. cellar   9. country
5. den   10. story

PAGE 25
1. forbids   6. grip
2. complain   7. mourn
3. bear   8. pay
4. allow   9. prevent
5. suggest   10. restore

PAGE 26
1. humid   6. Vigorous
2. petite   7. heavy
3. strict   8. clever
4. secret   9. weird
5. rude   10. brief

PAGE 27
1. tenaciously
2. tersely
3. noticeably
4. characteristically
5. severely
6. wistfully
7. shrewdly
8. covertly

PAGE 28
A. ACROSS: 3. abundance
   6. vision 7. strength
   DOWN: 1. precision
   2. validity 4. benefit
   5. crisis
B. 1. benefit   5. strength
   2. abundance 6. validity
   3. crisis   7. vision
   4. precision

PAGE 29
Sentences must include the noun:
1. variety
2. intelligence
3. repetition
4. pride
5. ruthlessness
6. loyalty
7. expression
8. heredity
9. futility
10. solemnity
11. eminence

PAGE 30
A. ACROSS: 2. prosperous
   5. satisfactory
   6. respectful
   DOWN: 1. perishable
   3. excellent 4. broken
B. 1. satisfactory
   2. prosperous
   3. broken
   4. perishable
   5. excellent
   6. respectful
C. Answers will vary.

PAGE 31
Sentences must include the adjective:
1. migratory
2. praiseworthy
3. emergent
4. tolerant
5. mournful
6. sewn
7. shady
8. persuasive
9. offensive
10. magnetic
11. informative

PAGE 32
A. ACROSS: 1. disrupt
   4. relieve 7. decide
   DOWN: 2. recover
   3. descend 5. invade
   6. collect
B. 1. descend   5. relieve
   2. invade   6. disrupt
   3. collect   7. decide
   4. recover

PAGE 33
Sentences must include the verb:
1. vacate   7. provide
2. apologize 8. economize
3. intervene 9. cite
4. examine   10. observe
5. comment   11. know
6. guide

PAGE 34
A. 2. peek, seek, week
   3. foil, toil, soil
   4. hire, fire, tire
   5. dart, part, tart
   6. toss, moss, boss
B. 1. chick, thick, quick
   2. dress, chess, guess
   3. plant, grant, slant
   4. brass, class, glass

PAGE 35
A. 1. t   3. s   5. f
   2. m   4. p   6. c
B. 1. t   3. d
   2. k   4. e
C. 2. club
   3. lint
   4. brag
   5. slay or stay
   6. fair
   7. scum
   8. hint or hilt

PAGE 36
A. 1. e / afternoon
   2. b / barefoot
   3. h / campfire
   4. l / daydream
   5. m / earring
   6. d / fireplace
   7. j / gentleman
   8. i / handlebar
   9. g / icepick
   10. k / jellyfish
   11. f / keepsake
   12. c / leftover
   13. a / motorcycle
B. Word choices and drawings will vary.

PAGE 37
A. 1. dragonfly
   2. popcorn
   3. newborn
   4. applesauce
   5. jackknife
   6. flashlight
   7. rainbow
   8. nightgown
B. ACROSS: 2. rowboat
   5. toenails 6. lipstick
   7. mailbox   8. vineyard
   DOWN: 1. greenhouse
   3. quicksand
   4. skateboard

PAGE 38
A. 1. g, indebted
   2. d, outlaw
   3. f, outlook
   4. c, inmate
   5. b, insight
   6. e, outrage
   7. a, outcast
B. ACROSS: 1. indoors
   3. ingrown 6. outburst
   7. invaluable
   DOWN: 2. outset
   4. outbreak 5. outdated

PAGE 39
1. inlet   7. instep
2. inseam   8. outfield
3. outgoing   9. outbound
4. outcome   10. outlet
5. invoice   11. inside,
6. instill   outside

PAGE 40
A. 1. uproot
   2. downstairs
   3. downfall
   4. upbeat
   5. downwind
   6. uproar
B. ACROSS: 1. upturn
   5. downpour 7. downcast
   8. upright   9. upkeep
   DOWN: 2. uprising
   3. downgrade 4. update
   6. downtown

PAGE 41
1. uplift   7. upfront
2. downhill   8. downright
3. upcoming   9. Downtrodden
4. upriver   10. upbringing
5. uphill
6. downhearted

PAGE 42
A. 1. b, underdog
   2. g, overthrow
   3. f, overcast
   4. c, underhanded
   5. a, undergraduate
   6. e, overhaul
   7. d, undertake
B. ACROSS: 1. overturn
   4. undergo 5. understand
   6. undermine
   DOWN: 1. overdue
   2. understudy 3. overcome

PAGE 43
1. overlook
2. underworld
3. overshadow
4. undertaker
5. overtime
6. undertow
7. overstock
8. overload
9. underfoot
10. underbrush
11. undertone

PAGE 44
A. Answers will vary. Possible answers.
3. G: oak, maple, etc.
4. G: dog, lion, etc.
5. G: wrench, pliers, etc.
6. S: fish
7. S: color
8. G: journal, paperback, *Black Beauty*, etc.
9. S: fabric
10. S: grain

B. Order of word pairs will vary.

MORE INTENSE	LESS INTENSE
2. obese	plump
3. frosty	cool
4. destroy	damage
5. gush	dribble
6. uproarious	amusing
7. brilliant	clever
8. revolting	unattractive
9. superb	satisfactory
10. outrageous	inappropriate

PAGE 45
Answers will vary.

PAGE 46
1. thermal
2. telescope
3. bigamy
4. aristocrat
5. telegraph
6. geology
7. Thermos
8. dialogue
9. metropolis
10. prologue
11. graphologist

PAGE 47
A. 1. c 3. d 5. a
      2. f 4. b 6. e
B. 1. fly
      2. book
      3. time
      4. water
C. Answers will vary. Possible answers:
      1. physique
      2. synonym
      3. mechanic
      4. photography

PAGE 48
1. vacation
2. verdict
3. temporary
4. auditorium
5. mortuary
6. audio-visual
7. certain
8. predict
9. science
10. contradict
11. certificate

PAGE 49
A. 1. feel   4. cut
      2. conquer 5. hold
      3. end   6. give
B. Answers will vary. Possible answers:
      1. novel   3. just
      2. memory 4. suicide

PAGE 50
1. magnifying
2. multiplication
3. misinformed
4. disobey
5. union
6. preamble
7. remind
8. discolored
9. misspell
10. uniform
11. postpone

PAGE 51
A. 1. distant 4. half
      2. two   5. into
      3. hundred 6. across
B. 1. un   4. un
      2. non 5. un
      3. Non 6. non

PAGE 52
1. boredom
2. insurance
3. hardship
4. anticipation
5. preparedness
6. application
7. employment
8. desperation
9. ownership
10. absence
11. Freedom

PAGE 53
A. 1. glorious
      2. fraudulent
      3. thoughtful
      4. comatose
      5. nervous
      6. turbulent
      7. successful
B. 1. heroism 4. thunder
      2. piracy   5. voyage
      3. parade   6. Racism

PAGE 54
1. cartoonist
2. pianist
3. biologist
4. electrician
5. editor
6. auditor
7. gardener
8. instructor
9. conductor
10. dietitian

PAGE 55
A. 1. pioneer
      2. financier
      3. lieutenant
      4. soldier
      5. recipient
      6. superintendent
      7. volunteer
B. 1. author
      2. locksmith
      3. mechanic
      4. chauffeur
      5. therapist
      6. playwright
      7. auctioneer
      8. politician
      9. surgeon
      10. astronomer
      11. cashier

PAGE 56
1. effect
2. morale
3. proceed
4. imminent
5. lapse
6. accept
7. dispersed
8. formerly
9. uninterested
10. dissent
11. disprove

PAGE 57
A. ACROSS: 1. relapse   6. disapprove   7. precede
      DOWN: 2. except   3. disburse   4. moral   5. descent
B. 1. f   4. h   7. i   10. g
      2. j   5. b   8. e
      3. a   6. c   9. d

PAGE 58
1. e, devil
2. d, submergence
3. f, facts
4. h, jurist
5. b, scoop
6. j, memento
7. c, pamphlet
8. a, liability
9. g, accomplishment
10. i, fortune

PAGE 59
1. beards   6. myths
2. chum   7. defect
3. belly   8. Market
4. copy   9. decency
5. cargo   10. history

PAGE 60
A. 1. explain   6. quit
      2. exchange   7. accuse
      3. bother   8. worry
      4. teach   9. send
      5. win

B. 1. converse, communicate
      2. acclaim, commend
      3. support, substantiate
      4. gather, accumulate
      5. reclaim, seize
      6. beguile, amuse
      7. ooze, seep
      8. begin, initiate
      9. weep, sob

PAGE 61
A. 1. rot   4. fly
      2. escape   5. finish
      3. steal   6. eat
B. Answers will vary. Possible answers:
      1. fix   4. assist
      2. try   5. labor
      3. respond   6. forecast
C. Sentences will vary but should include appropriate synonyms for:
      cheat (trick, fool, swindle)
      smile (grin, smirk)
      stare (look, peer)
      quarrel (fight, argue)
      laugh (giggle, chuckle)
      hate (despise, dislike)
      donate (give, contribute)

PAGE 62
1. e, impartial
2. f, erroneous
3. g, horrendous
4. b, obstinate
5. h, theatrical
6. i, dismal
7. j, normal
8. c, evident
9. a, vigilant
10. d, ridiculous

PAGE 63
A. 1. likeable, nice
      2. swift, quick
      3. perpetual, endless
      4. main, major
      5. peculiar, unusual
      6. garish, showy
      7. ineffective, useless
      8. persuasive, compelling
B. Answers will vary. Possible answers:
      1. hard, tough
      2. right, true, factual
      3. big, huge, gigantic
      4. wordy, unending
      5. cheerful, gay, chipper
      6. good, flavorful, scrumptious, yummy

PAGE 64
A. 1. c 3. f 5. b 7. h
      2. e 4. a 6. d 8. g
B. ACROSS: 1. fondly   4. almost   5. wildly   7. sometimes
      DOWN: 1. forward   2. rarely   3. somewhat   4. now

PAGE 65

	SCRAMBLE	CIRCLE
1.	promptly	immediately
2.	rather	quite
3.	very	especially
4.	lately	recently
5.	well	satisfactorily
6.	suddenly	abruptly
7.	fairly	pretty
8.	much	often
9.	more	again
10.	further	more

PAGE 66
A. 1. c 4. b 7. i 10. g
  2. d 5. a 8. l 11. h
  3. f 6. e 9. k 12. j
B. 1. democracy
  2. similarity
  3. generosity
  4. celebrity
  5. mansion
  6. criticism
  7. guilt
  8. betrayal
C. Sentences will vary.
  1. sanity   3. reward
  2. defense   4. victory

PAGE 67
A. Sequence will vary.
  1. death / birth
  2. luck / misfortune
  3. amateur / professional
  4. modesty / conceit
  5. success / failure
  6. ceiling / floor
  7. height / depth
  8. recovery / relapse
  9. intelligence / stupidity
  10. reduction / enlargement
  11. hypocrisy / sincerity
  12. beginner / veteran
  13. fiction / fact
  14. certainty / doubt
B. ACROSS: 1. leader 5. entry
  7. absence 8. ally
  DOWN: 2. dwarf 3. mountain
  4. genius 6. fantasy

PAGE 68
1. fortify   6. minimize
2. repulsed   7. sterilized
3. hoard   8. liberate
4. demand   9. enhanced
5. allow

PAGE 69
A. 1. shout   6. reveal
  2. laugh   7. apply
  3. perish   8. forget
  4. freeze   9. lower
  5. answer   10. ascend
B. ACROSS: 2. praise 4. halve
  6. admit 7. retreat
  DOWN: 1. select 3. reveal
  4. halt 5. smile

PAGE 70
A. 1. stale
  2. biased
  3. critical
  4. complex
  5. humble
  6. comic
  7. scrawny
  8. boisterous
B. 1. vulnerable
  2. exciting
  3. superior
  4. unusual
  5. flexible
  6. immaculate
  7. punctual
  8. feasible

PAGE 71
A. 1. false   6. straight
  2. sweet   7. entire
  3. genuine   8. severe
  4. better   9. rough
  5. perfect   10. normal
B. ACROSS: 1. hairy 3. attractive
  6. idle 7. lost 8. easy
  DOWN: 1. harmful 2. retail
  4. vacant 5. flimsy

PAGE 72
A. 1. severely
  2. repeatedly
  3. eventually
  4. rudely
  5. artificially
  6. eagerly
  7. initially
  8. up
  9. irregularly
B. ACROSS: 3. never 4. yesterday
  5. afterward 7. sincerely
  DOWN: 1. more 2. there
  3. nowhere 6. then

PAGE 73
A. Sequence will vary.
  1. partially / wholly
  2. illegally / lawfully
  3. cautiously / recklessly
  4. vigorously / lazily
  5. calmly / frantically
  6. keenly / mildly
  7. firmly / loosely
  8. secretly / openly
  9. somewhere / nowhere
  10. generally / specifically
B. ACROSS: 4. early 6. weakly
  8. now 9. yesterday
  10. carefully
  DOWN: 1. always
  2. generally 3. slowly
  5. warmly 7. poorly

PAGE 74
A. 1. herd   6. ate
  2. sale   7. hare
  3. doe   8. soar
  4. or   9. steal
  5. miner
B. ACROSS: 2. bridle 5. guest
  6. not 8. flour 10. tow
  11. whole
  DOWN: 1. plain 3. rows
  4. hour 7. threw
  8. fowl 9. new
C.
	CIRCLE	REPLACE WITH
1.	ewe	you
	air	heir
	grate	great
2.	Eye	I
	bare's	bear's
	clause	claws
3.	Wood	Would
	lone	loan
	sum	some

PAGE 75
A. 1. hare hair
  2. whale wail
  3. plain plane
  4. minor miner
  5. foul fowl
  6. ant aunt
  7. male mail
B. 1. bolder boulder
  2. real reel
  3. bored board
  4. sole soul
  5. capitol capital
  6. better bettor

PAGE 76
A. 1. bark   5. lean
  2. hide   6. mine
  3. palm   7. sole
  4. loaf   8. like
B. RIDDLE ANSWER: spelling
  1. husky   5. troll
  2. pound   6. miss
  3. lead   7. prune
  4. vault   8. light

PAGE 77
A. Definitions will vary.
  1. eight: the number after seven
  2. tacks: short, sharp-pointed nails
  3. one: a single thing or unit
  4. weak: lacking in strength
  5. rap: to tap, or a kind of music
  6. hire: to employ for wages
  7. two: the number following one;
     —or—
     to: in a direction toward
  8. wheel: a round disk that turns on an axle
B. Answers will vary, but sentences should reflect word meanings and part of speech.

PAGE 78
1. a 3. a 5. b 7. b
2. b 4. a 6. b 8. a

PAGE 79
A. 1. b 3. d 5. c
  2. f 4. a 6. e
B. 1. as soon as possible
  2. government issue
  3. random-access memory
  4. save our ship
  5. Ku Klux Klan
  6. National Socialist German Workers' Party
C. ACROSS: 2. SALT 3. NASA
  4. FDA 6. OPEC 8. IRS
  9. SSA
  DOWN: 1. OSHA 3. NATO
  4. FBI 5. OAS 7. CIA

PAGE 80
A. 1. carbohydrates
  2. limousine
  3. representative
  4. veteran
  5. dormitory
  6. hamburger
  7. refrigerator
  8. laboratory
B. 1. bike   5. ump
  2. gas   6. perp
  3. tux   7. champ
  4. cab/taxi 8. grad

PAGE 81
A. ACROSS: 1. airplane
  4. fanatic 7. convict
  8. gymnasium
  DOWN: 2. influenza
  3. market 5. teenager
  6. mistress
B. 1. referee
  2. memorandum
  3. mathematics examination
  4. popular
  5. Labrador
  6. executive, professor

PAGE 82
A. 1. eyes   6. heart
  2. poisons   7. nerves
  3. mind   8. kidneys
  4. women   9. diseases
  5. skin   10. drugs
B. ACROSS: 1. words
  5. earthquakes 6. hearing
  9. society 10. birds
  DOWN: 2. snakes 3. fossils
  4. weather 7. insects
  8. God

PAGE 83
1. b 3. b 5. c 7. a
2. c 4. a 6. b 8. b

PAGE 84
1. b 3. c 5. b 7. c
2. a 4. a 6. a

PAGE 85
1. g 4. h 7. d 10. e
2. f 5. j 8. c 11. b
3. a 6. i 9. l 12. k

PAGE 86
A. 1. f 3. g 5. c 7. e
   2. a 4. b 6. h 8. d
B. 1. a 3. c 5. b
   2. b 4. a

PAGE 87
1. took up
2. put off
3. back up
4. pull off
5. ran through
6. fall back on
7. carry on
8. take on
9. let on
10. drop over

PAGE 88
1. b 3. a 5. a 7. c
2. a 4. c 6. b 8. a

PAGE 89
1. b 3. c 5. b 7. b
2. a 4. b 6. b 8. a

PAGE 90
1. b 4. c 7. a 9. a
2. b 5. b 8. c 10. b
3. a 6. b

PAGE 91
A. 1. goose   4. shoot
   2. thumbs   5. bull
   3. beat
B. 1. c 3. a 5. b
   2. e 4. d

PAGE 92
1. b 3. c 5. a 7. a
2. a 4. b 6. c 8. b

PAGE 93
1. beat the rap; threw the book at him
2. all in the same boat; give them the axe
3. blowing his top; mend fences
4. pass the buck; face the music
5. in the bag; eat crow
6. put much stock in; talk out of both sides of her mouth
7. bring home the bacon; keep the wolf from the door

PAGE 94
1. nib   7. ebb
2. irk   8. opt
3. urn   9. yen
4. apt   10. pry
5. eke   11. spa
6. hex

PAGE 95
Sentences will vary, but confirm that assigned word has been used properly.

PAGE 96
1. trek   7. vile
2. raze   8. cede
3. rout   9. shun
4. abet   10. deem
5. tuft   11. skew
6. idle

PAGE 97
Sentences will vary, but confirm that assigned word has been used properly.

PAGE 98
1. tunic   6. acute
2. girth   7. proxy
3. plush   8. farce
4. allay   9. debit
5. elegy 10. pithy

PAGE 99
Sentences will vary, but confirm that assigned word has been used properly.

PAGE 100
1. pundit   7. qualms
2. baffle   8. hearty
3. dawdle   9. fidget
4. affirm 10. carafe
5. defame 11. finale
6. sensor

PAGE 101
Sentences will vary, but confirm that assigned word has been used properly.

PAGE 102
1. bonanza   7. oppress
2. terrain   8. fervent
3. vintage   9. tedious
4. platoon 10. Geology
5. gesture 11. textile
6. subsist

PAGE 103
Sentences will vary, but confirm that assigned word has been used properly.

PAGE 104
1. eligible   7. virulent
2. skirmish   8. suffrage
3. isolated   9. genocide
4. monetary 10. latitude
5. parallel 11. alliance
6. retrieve

PAGE 105
Sentences will vary, but confirm that assigned word has been used properly.

PAGE 106
1. improvise   7. ambitious
2. tolerance   8. stalemate
3. menagerie   9. repellent
4. outspoken 10. Migratory
5. sophomore 11. dissuade
6. tradition

PAGE 107
Sentences will vary, but confirm that assigned word has been used properly.

PAGE 108
1. irrational
2. vocational
3. evaluation
4. pharmacist
5. Futuristic
6. appreciate
7. preference
8. Unforeseen
9. scandalous
10. Efficiency
11. indication

PAGE 109
Sentences will vary, but confirm that assigned word has been used properly.

PAGE 110
1. dilapidated
2. Elimination
3. predictable
4. partnership
5. monstrosity
6. bittersweet
7. spectacular
8. documentary
9. overwhelmed
10. insensitive
11. association

PAGE 111
Sentences will vary, but confirm that assigned word has been used properly.

PAGE 112
1. relationship
2. manufacturer
3. civilization
4. announcement
5. postponement
6. conservative
7. Emancipation
8. appendectomy, excruciating
9. illustration
10. anticipation
11. Constitution

PAGE 113
Sentences will vary, but confirm that assigned word has been used properly.

PAGE 114
1. Environmental
2. uncomfortable
3. controversial
4. determination
5. predominantly
6. justification
7. irresponsible
8. approximately
9. Revolutionary
10. demonstration
11. establishment

PAGE 115
Sentences will vary, but confirm that assigned word has been used properly.

PAGE 116
Approximate answers:
1. A hippodrome is an oval track once used for horse racing.
2. A jowl is the flesh under the lower jaw, especially when very loose.
3. A coati is a small animal that lives in trees in Mexico and South America.
4. A llama is a South American mammal; a llano is a grassy plain in South America.
5. A pulpit is where a clergyman stands to give a sermon.
6. A girl on a gurney (a wheeled cot used in the hospital) is probably injured or sick.
7. Marmots are small, burrowing animals with bushy tails.
8. The ozone layer in the atmosphere protects life on Earth.

PAGE 117
Approximate answers:
1. An automaton, a robot-like machine, would make the best servant. An autocrat is a dictator with complete power.
2. Since a misanthrope hates and distrusts all people, he would be more likely to be a hermit. A megalomaniac is one who craves power over other people.
3. Since pulchritude is physical beauty and pusillanimous means cowardly, I would rather be known as pulchritudinous.
4. Since fish is a major ingredient in bouillabaisse, inlanders would probably eat more vichyssoise, which is potato soup.
5. Troglodytes live in caves. Spelunkers explore caves as a hobby or pastime.
6. Lassitude is weariness to the point of losing interest in things. Turpitude means wickedness.

PAGE 118
ACROSS:
1. irony
4. symbol
6. tone
10. conflict
12. dialogue
13. mood
14. character
15. theme
16. novel
17. plot
18. moral

DOWN:
2. resolution
3. setting
4. style
5. climax
7. narrator
8. fiction
9. author
11. voice

PAGE 119
1. conflict
2. author
3. resolution
4. moral
5. novel
6. plot
7. setting
8. voice
9. narrator
10. character
11. dialogue
12. symbol

PAGE 120
ACROSS:
2. embryo
3. gestation
7. hormones
9. chromosomes
12. spine
13. reflex
14. artery
15. genes
16. anatomy
17. veins

DOWN:
1. femur
4. aorta
5. biceps
6. heart
7. heredity
8. organs
10. senses
11. brain

PAGE 121
1. brain
2. spine
3. anatomy
4. gestation
5. femur
6. organs
7. hormones
8. genes
9. heredity
10. Chromosomes
11. biceps

PAGE 122
ACROSS:
1. strait
6. delta
7. reef
9. Arctic
11. hemisphere
13. erosion
14. mesa
16. gulf
17. basin
18. monsoon

DOWN:
1. savanna
2. isthmus
3. peninsula
4. steppe
5. glacier
8. famine
10. tropics
12. reservoir
15. jungle

PAGE 123
1. Gulf
2. glacier
3. erosion
4. Hemisphere
5. Isthmus
6. basin
7. monsoon
8. tropics
9. Strait
10. savanna
11. steppe
12. peninsula

PAGE 124
ACROSS:
2. conservation
5. typhoon
7. climate
9. fossil
12. environment
13. core
14. atmosphere
16. astronomy
17. galaxy
18. condensation

DOWN:
1. orbit
2. continents
3. era
4. eclipse
6. planets
8. geology
10. ozone
11. meteor
13. crust
15. oceans

PAGE 125
1. continents
2. oceans
3. crust
4. planets
5. Era
6. condensation
7. climate
8. meteor
9. core
10. geology
11. galaxy

PAGE 126
ACROSS:
1. battery
5. elements
7. machine
8. properties
10. force
12. gravity
14. liquid
16. atoms
17. spectrum
18. chemistry
19. magnet

DOWN:
2. technology
3. matter
4. solid
6. energy
9. physics
10. friction
11. prism
13. vacuum
15. gas

PAGE 127
1. friction
2. elements
3. gas
4. battery
5. machine
6. energy
7. Gravity
8. matter
9. spectrum
10. solid
11. magnet
12. technology

PAGE 128
ACROSS:
2. ancestors
3. preamble
9. pioneers
11. tax
12. colonies
15. conquistadors
16. revolution
18. doctrine
19. suburbs
20. militia

DOWN:
1. patriots
4. abolition
5. buffalo
6. prairies
7. frontier
8. democracy
10. immigrants
13. economy
14. protest
17. rebel

PAGE 129
1. pioneers, prairies
2. buffalo
3. patriots
4. Revolution
5. immigrants
6. conquistadors
7. colonies
8. Abolition
9. Doctrine
10. protest, tax
11. militia

PAGE 130
ACROSS:
3. Holocaust
6. truce
9. pharaoh
10. medieval
12. treaty
13. apartheid
15. scribe
16. mummy
17. civilization
18. archeologist

DOWN:
1. philosophers
2. toga
4. serfs
5. nomads
7. castes
8. pictograms
9. plague
11. republic
14. empire

PAGE 131
1. pharaoh
2. medieval, serfs
3. philosophers
4. toga
5. treaty
6. plague
7. nomads
8. republic
9. Holocaust
10. civilization
11. apartheid
12. pictograms

PAGE 132
ACROSS:
1. perspective
5. watercolors
12. sketch
14. landscape
16. artist
17. oils
18. fresco
19. palette
20. gallery

DOWN:
2. clay
3. portrait
4. sculpture
6. etch
7. museum
8. design
9. model
10. charcoal
11. marble
13. easel
15. canvas

PAGE 133
1. sculpture
2. sketch
3. gallery
4. museum
5. palette
6. easel
7. watercolors
8. oils
9. portrait
10. marble
11. artist

PAGE 134
ACROSS:
4. paraphrase
8. effect
12. formulate
13. justify
14. summarize
15. interpret
16. analyze
17. estimate

DOWN:
1. rank
2. trace
3. general
5. specify
6. cite
7. discuss
9. outline
10. predict
11. relate

PAGE 135
1. analyze
2. discuss
3. Trace
4. rank
5. effect
6. estimate
7. Interpret
8. cite
9. summarize
10. outline
11. predict